Classic and Contemporary Disney Hits

1

**Arranged by
Nancy and Randall Faber**

Production Coordinator: Jon Ophoff
Cover: Terpstra Design, San Francisco
Engraving: Dovetree Productions, Inc.

Disney Characters and Artwork © Disney

FABER
PIANO ADVENTURES®

HAL•LEONARD®

ISBN 978-1-61677-238-3

Printed in U.S.A.

FOREWORD

Disney songs connect a generation. And special songs take us back to special moments. This book invites you to reconnect to those melodies and times at the piano. You'll find beloved Disney songs from a wide array of movies such as *Aladdin, Beauty and the Beast, Coco, Frozen, The Lion King, The Little Mermaid, Mary Poppins, Mulan,* and more!

Adult Piano Adventures® Disney Book 1 is designed for adult beginners and for those who have played piano in the past and are reacquainting with the keyboard. Those exploring the piano for the first time will find the arrangements appealing and well within reach. Adults returning to the keyboard can "brush up on basics" while exploring timeless hits and popular favorites.

This book has three sections.

- Section 1 features piano arrangements with **minimal hand position changes**. Many Disney selections include an optional duet part. In Section 1, hand shifts are routinely shown with a circled finger number and the word "shift" or "move." These cues alert players to important movements of the hand.

- Section 2 introduces the key of **C major** with the **one-octave scale** for each hand, and **I, IV,** and **V7 chords**. With these three chords, a pianist can play many of Disney's most famous hits. In Section 2, the word "shift" again alerts hand movements. Usually when the same passage is repeated, the word "shift" is not included. Circled finger numbers are not featured.

- Section 3 introduces the key of **G major** with the **one-octave scale** for each hand, and **I, IV,** and **V7 chords**. Blockbuster Disney tunes in the key of G follow. In Section 3, the word "shift" and circled finger numbers are not included for full independent reading and as preparation for **Adult Piano Adventures® Disney** Book 2.

TABLE OF CONTENTS

SECTION 1: BEGINNING DISNEY SONGS
Easy arrangements with simple harmonies

Do You Want to Build a Snowman? (from *Frozen*) 4
I See the Light (from *Tangled*) 6
Step in Time (from *Mary Poppins*). 8
Part of Your World (from *The Little Mermaid*) 10
It's a Small World (from Disney Parks' "it's a small world" Attraction). . . 12
A Spoonful of Sugar (from *Mary Poppins*) 14
Let's Go Fly a Kite (from *Mary Poppins*) 16
Gaston (from *Beauty and the Beast*) 18
Remember Me (Ernesto de la Cruz) (from *Coco*) 22
Chim Chim Cher-ee (from *Mary Poppins*) 24
He's a Pirate (from *Pirates of the Caribbean*) 26

SECTION 2: DISNEY SONGS IN THE KEY OF C MAJOR
(with I, IV, and V7 chords)

Introduction to the Key of C 28
The Bare Necessities (from *The Jungle Book*) 29
Supercalifragilisticexpialidocious (from *Mary Poppins*) 32
Scales and Arpeggios (from *The Aristocats*) 34
A Whole New World (from *Aladdin*) 36
Colors of the Wind (from *Pocahontas*) 39
Be Our Guest (from *Beauty and the Beast*) 42
Belle (from *Beauty and the Beast*) 44
Let It Go (from *Frozen*) 46
I've Got a Dream (from *Tangled*) 49

SECTION 3: DISNEY SONGS IN THE KEY OF G MAJOR
(with I, IV, and V7 chords)

Introduction to the Key of G 52
I Just Can't Wait to Be King (from *The Lion King*) 53
Under the Sea (from *The Little Mermaid*). 56
Bella Notte (from *Lady and the Tramp*) 58
Reflection (from *Mulan*). 60
Can You Feel the Love Tonight (from *The Lion King*). 62
Circle of Life (from *The Lion King*) 65
Proud Corazón (from *Coco*). 68
Fathoms Below (from *The Little Mermaid*) 72
Beauty and the Beast (from *Beauty and the Beast*). 74

Dictionary of Musical Terms 78
Alphabetical Index of Titles. 80

Do You Want to Build a Snowman?

from *Frozen*

**Music and Lyrics by
Kristen Anderson-Lopez
and Robert Lopez**

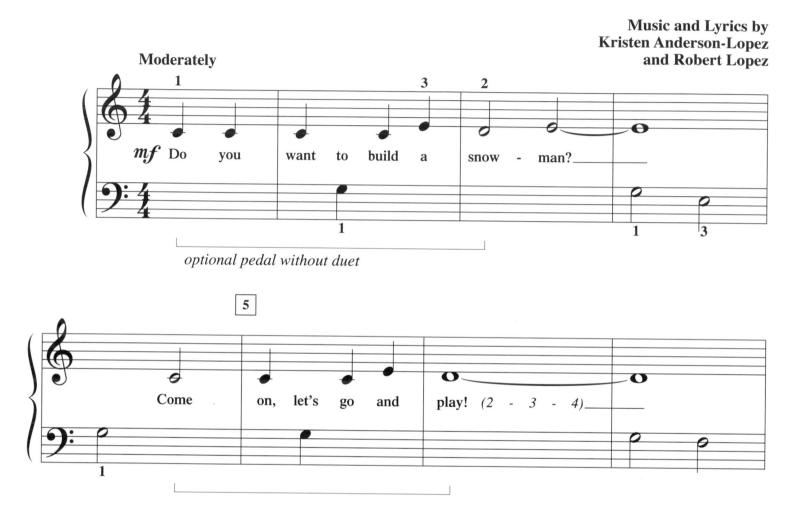

optional pedal without duet

Teacher Duet: (Student plays 1 octave higher)

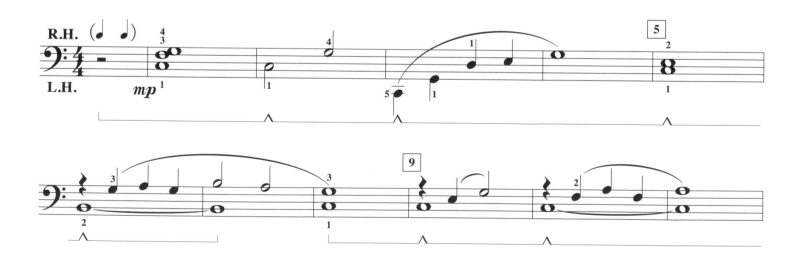

I See the Light

from *Tangled*

Music by Alan Menken
Lyrics by Glenn Slater

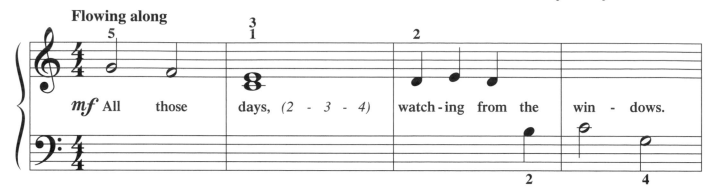

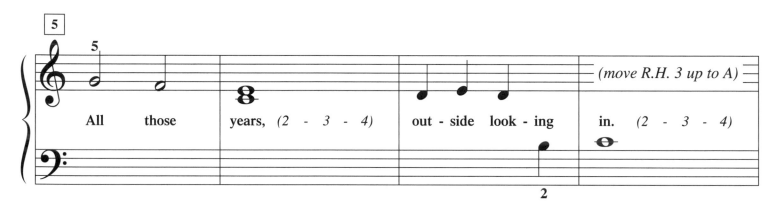

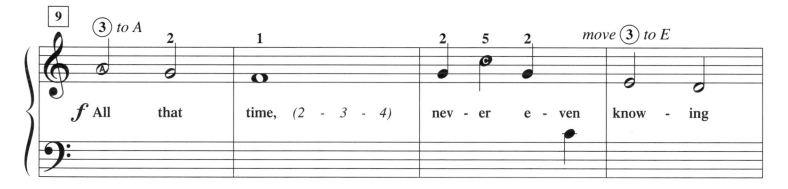

Teacher Duet: (Student plays 1 octave higher)

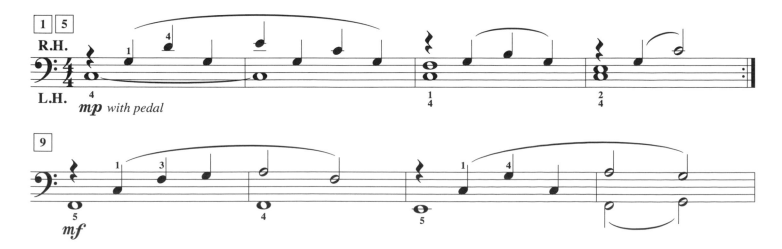

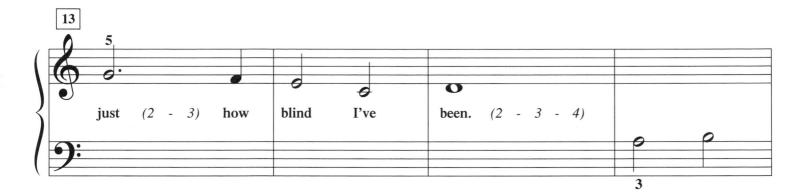

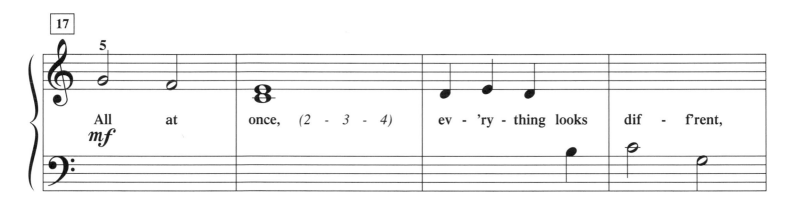

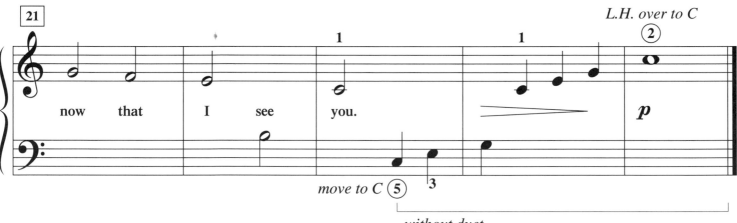

Step in Time
from *Mary Poppins*

**Words and Music by
Richard M. Sherman
and Robert B. Sherman**

With spirit

mf Kick your knees up, step in time! Kick your knees up, step in time!

Never need (a) rea - son, never need (a) rhyme, Kick your knees up, step in time!

mf Round the chim - ney, step in time! Round the chim - ney, step in time!

Teacher Duet: (Student plays 1 octave higher)

R.H.

L.H. *mp*

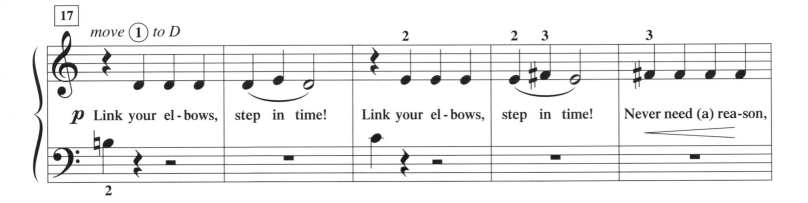

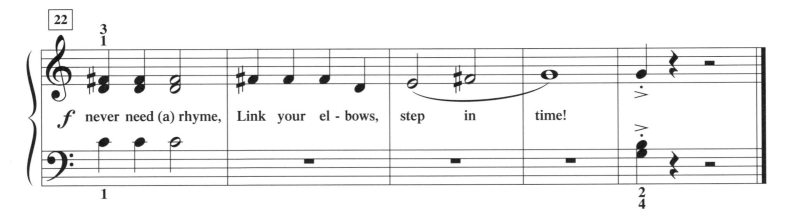

Part of Your World
from *The Little Mermaid*

Music by Alan Menken
Lyrics by Howard Ashman

Teacher Duet: (Student plays 1 octave higher)

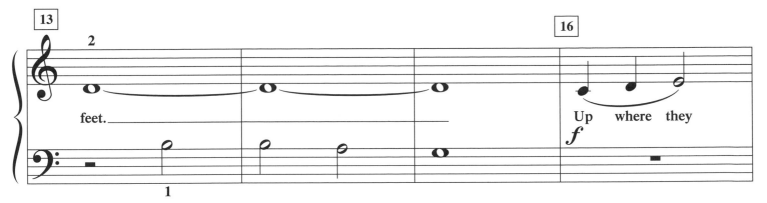

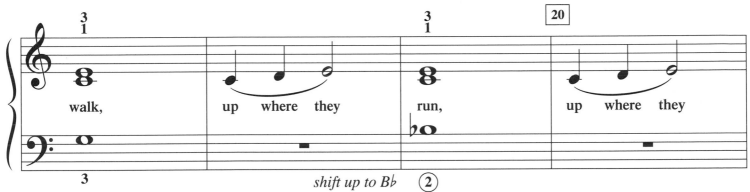

feet.

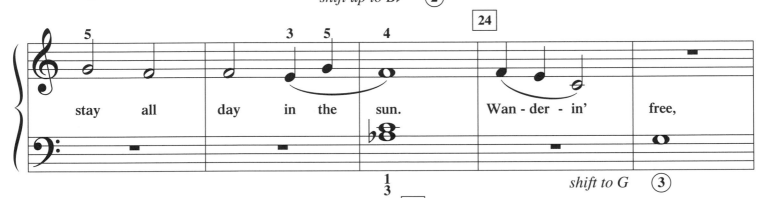

walk, up where they run, up where they

shift up to B♭ ②

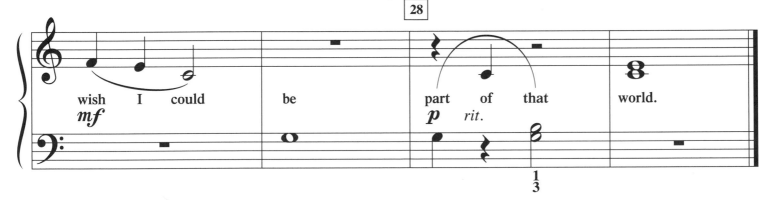

stay all day in the sun. Wan - der - in' free,

shift to G ③

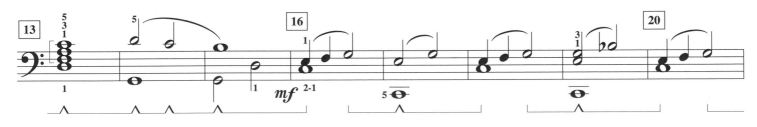

wish I could be part of that world.

mf *p* *rit.*

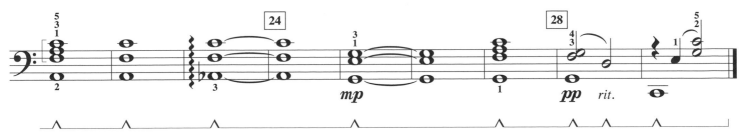

It's a Small World

from Disney Parks' "it's a small world" Attraction

Words and Music by
Richard M. Sherman
and Robert B. Sherman

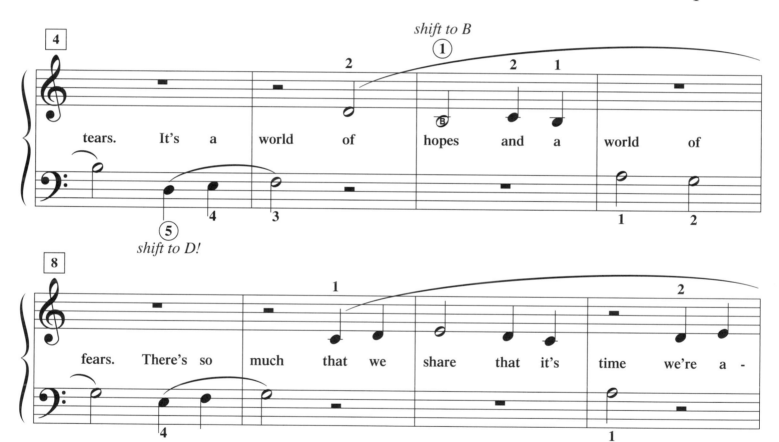

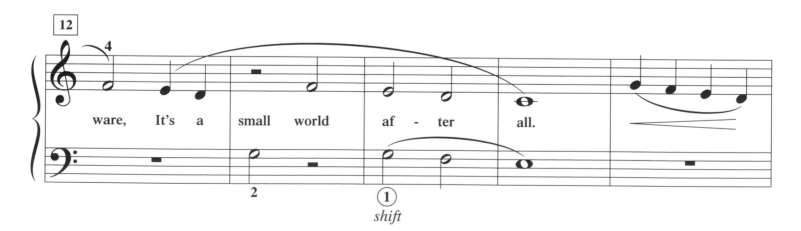

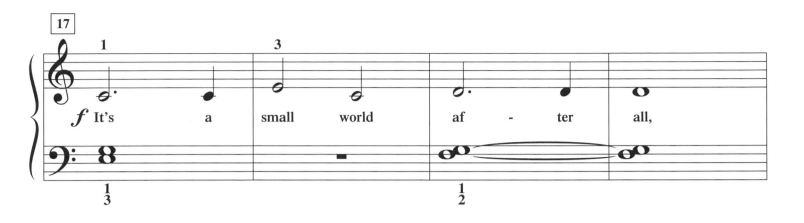

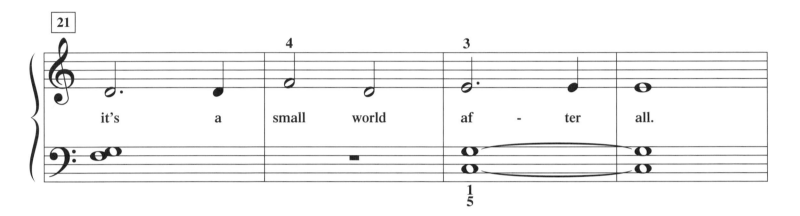

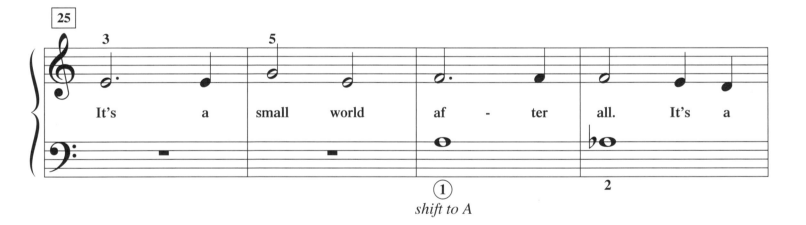

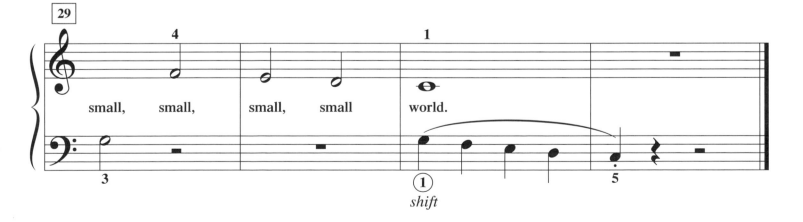

A Spoonful of Sugar

from *Mary Poppins*

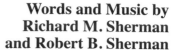

Words and Music by
Richard M. Sherman
and Robert B. Sherman

Cheerfully

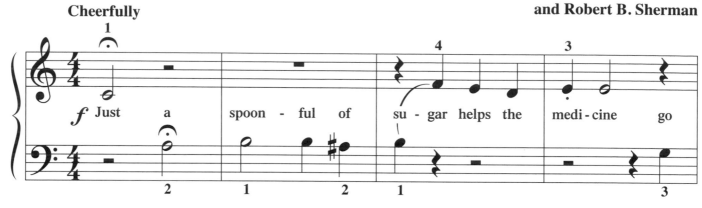

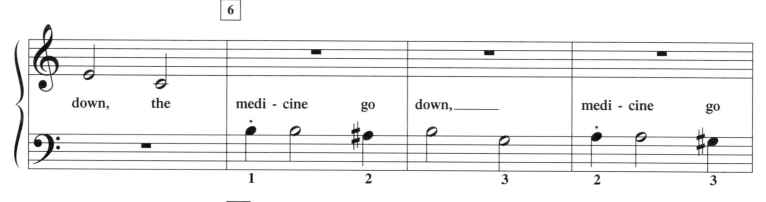

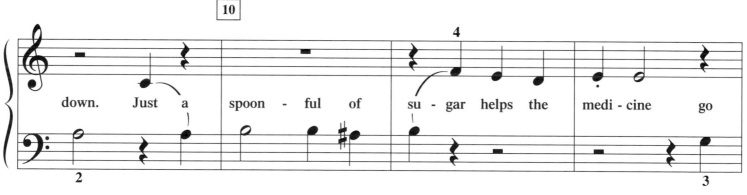

Teacher Duet: (Student plays 1 octave higher)

© 1963 Wonderland Music Company, Inc.
Copyright Renewed.
All Rights Reserved. Used by Permission.

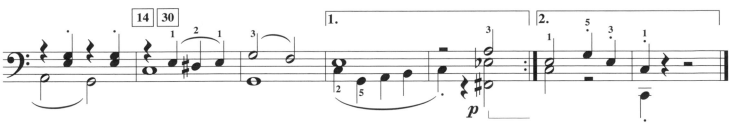

Let's Go Fly a Kite

from *Mary Poppins*

**Words and Music by
Richard M. Sherman
and Robert B. Sherman**

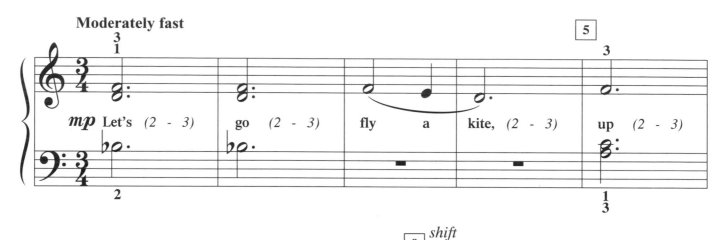

mp Let's (2 - 3) go (2 - 3) fly a kite, (2 - 3) up (2 - 3)

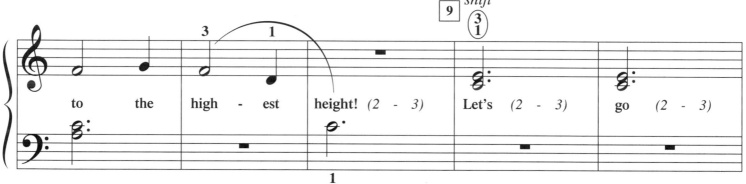

to the high - est height! (2 - 3) Let's (2 - 3) go (2 - 3)

Teacher Duet: (Student plays 1 octave higher)

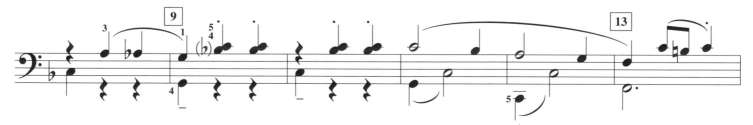

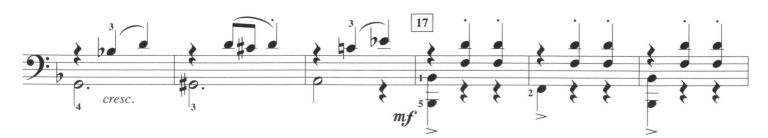

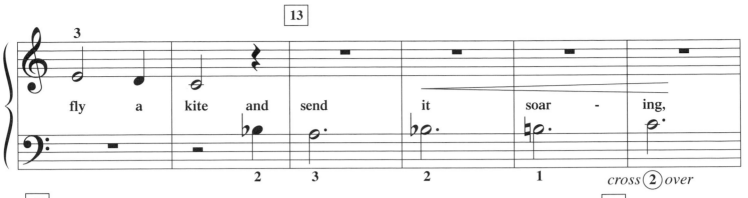

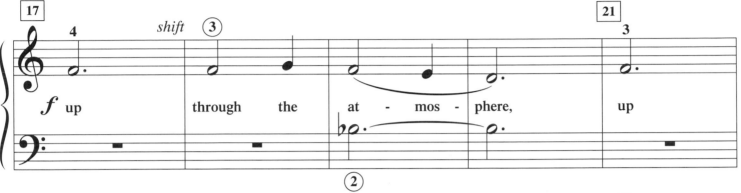

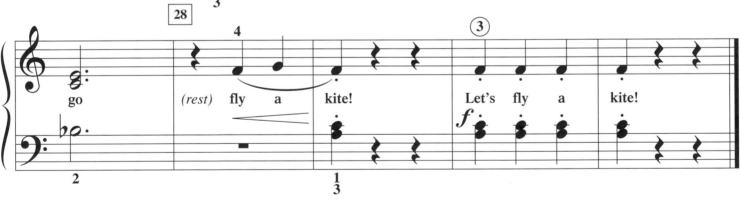

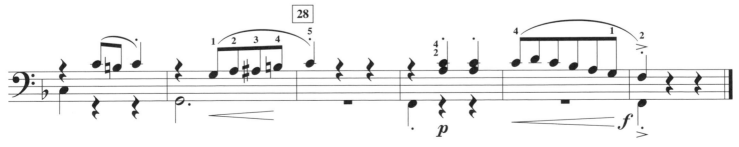

Gaston

from *Beauty and the Beast*

Music by Alan Menken
Lyrics by Howard Ashman

Teacher Duet: (Student plays 1 octave higher)

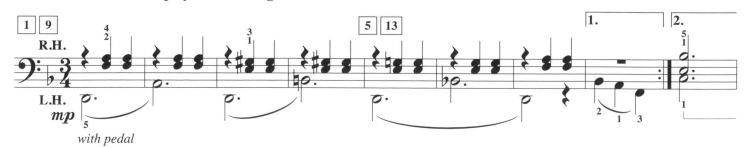

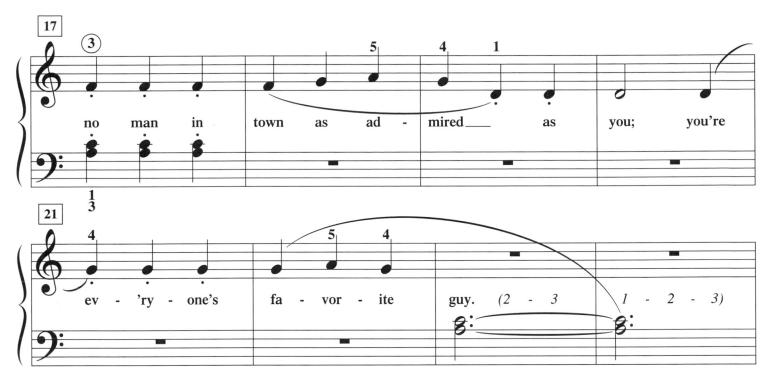

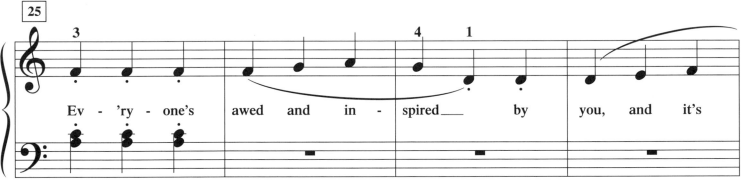

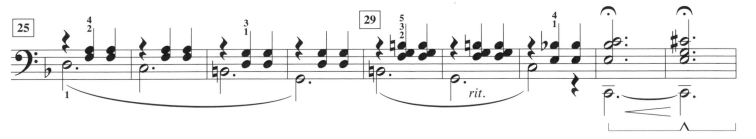

20

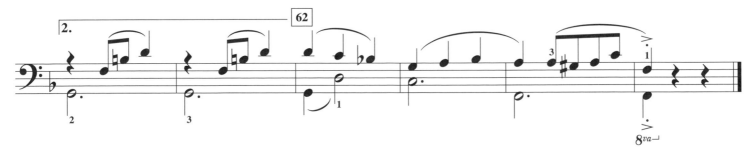

Remember Me

(Ernesto de la Cruz)
from Coco

**Words and Music by
Kristen Anderson-Lopez
and Robert Lopez**

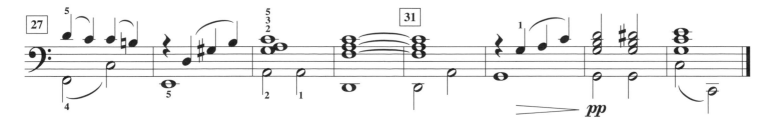

Chim Chim Cher-ee

from *Mary Poppins*

Words and Music by
Richard M. Sherman
and Robert B. Sherman

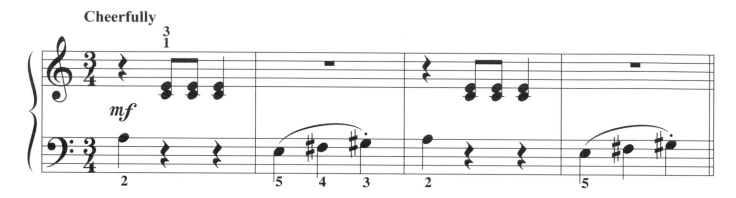

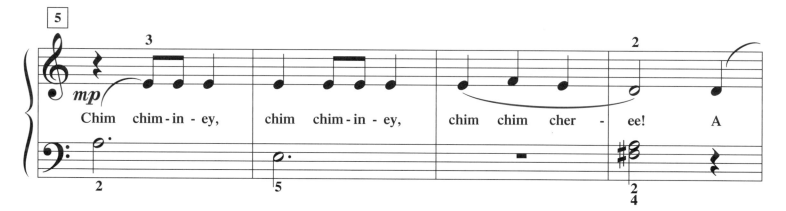

Teacher Duet: (Student plays 1 octave higher)

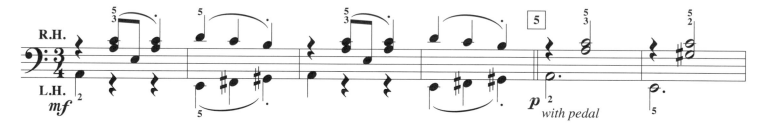

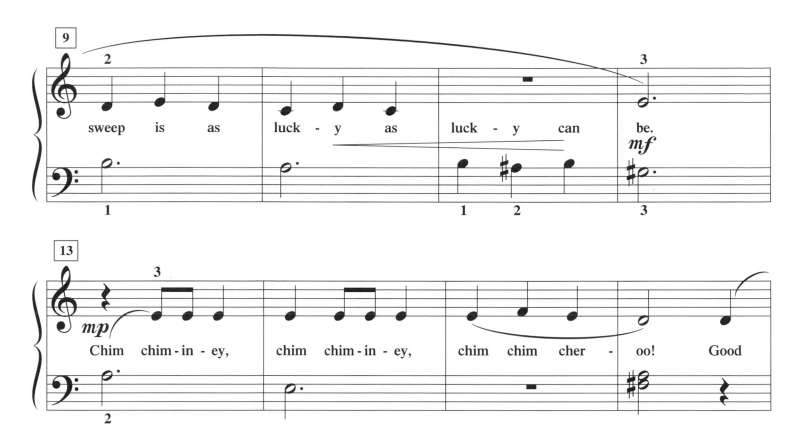

sweep is as luck - y as luck - y can be.

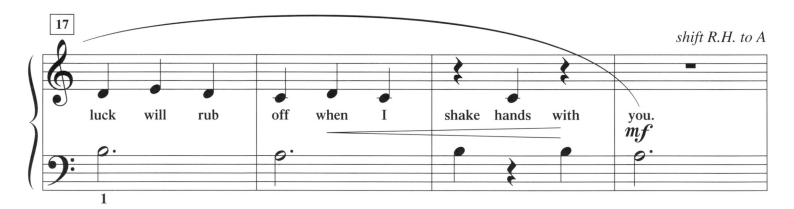

Chim chim-in-ey, chim chim-in-ey, chim chim cher-oo! Good

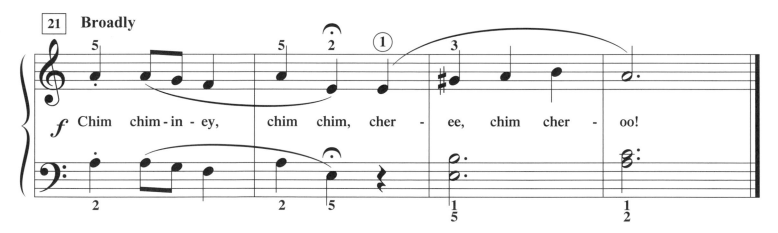

shift R.H. to A

luck will rub off when I shake hands with you.

Broadly

Chim chim-in-ey, chim chim, cher-ee, chim cher-oo!

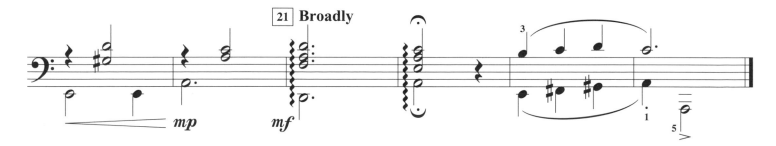

Broadly

He's a Pirate

from *Pirates of the Caribbean:*
The Curse of the Black Pearl

Music by Klaus Badelt,
Geoffrey Zanelli
and Hans Zimmer

With energy

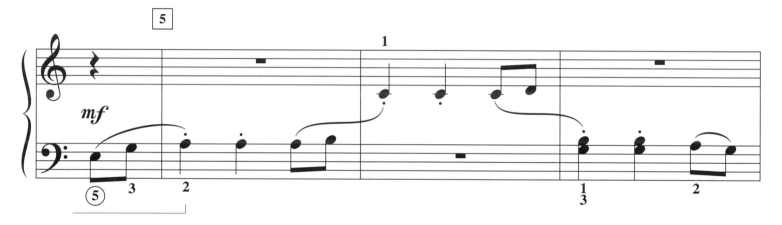

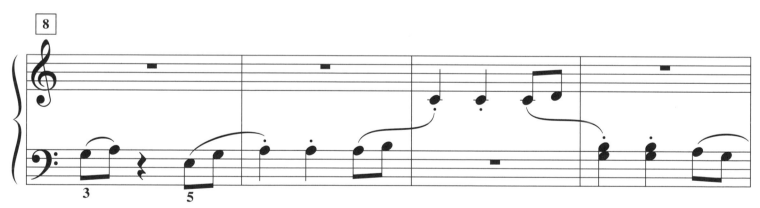

FF3060

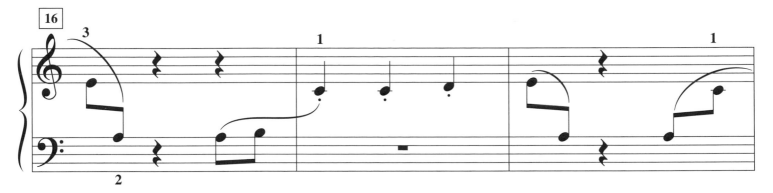

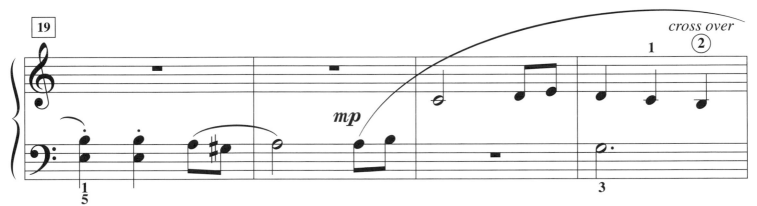

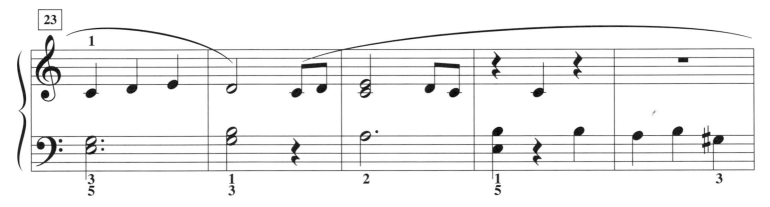

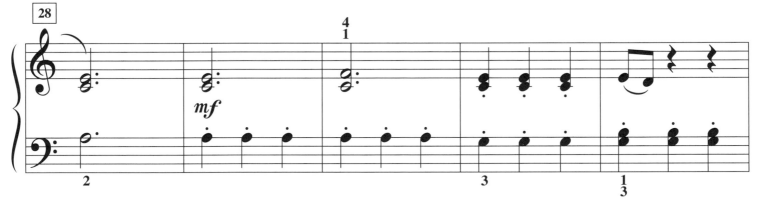

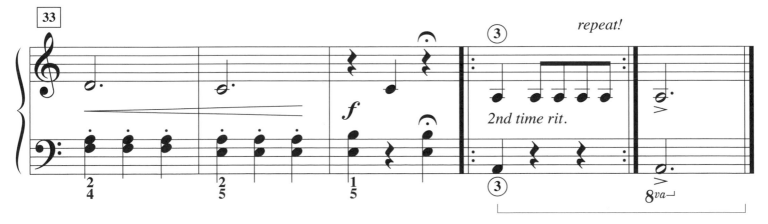

KEY OF C

C Major Scale

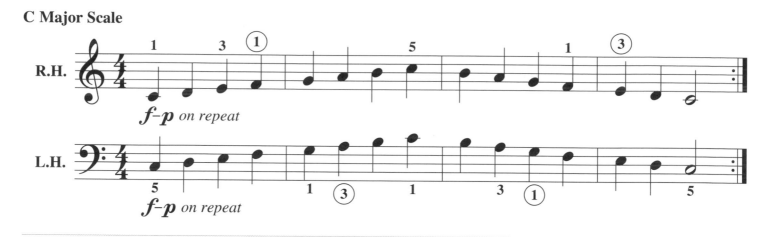

R.H.

f-*p* on repeat

L.H.

f-*p* on repeat

Primary Chords

The **I**, **IV**, and **V** chords are called the *primary chords*.
They are built on scale degrees 1, 4, and 5 of the major scale.

chord letter names: **C**   **F**   **G**

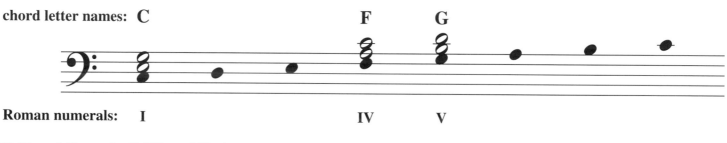

Roman numerals: **I**   **IV**   **V**

C, **F**, and **G** are the **I**, **IV**, and **V** chords in the Key of C.

Common Chord Positions

The chords above are shown in the *root position*, built up in 3rds from the chord *root* (chord name).
By inverting the notes, the **I**, **IV**, and **V7** chords can be played with little motion of the hand.

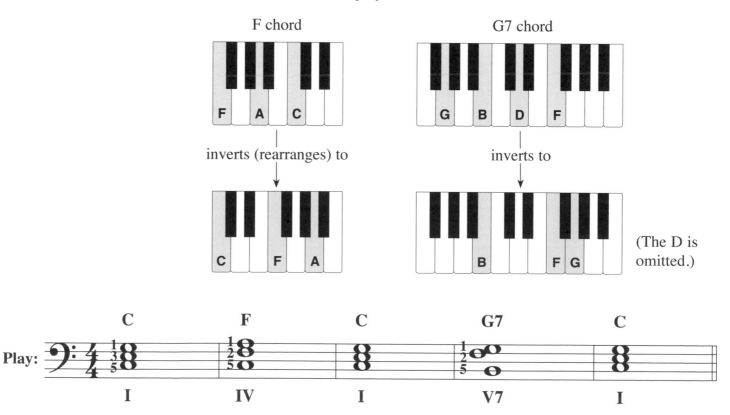

F chord   G7 chord

inverts (rearranges) to   inverts to

(The D is omitted.)

Play: C   F   C   G7   C

         I   IV   I   V7   I

The Bare Necessities

from *The Jungle Book*

**Words and Music by
Terry Gilkyson**

Bright and snappy

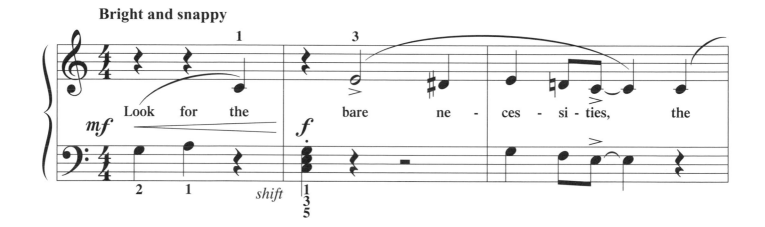

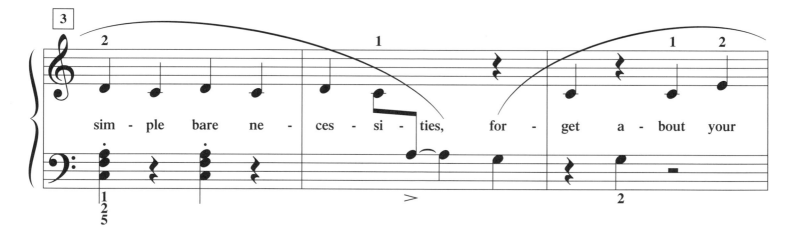

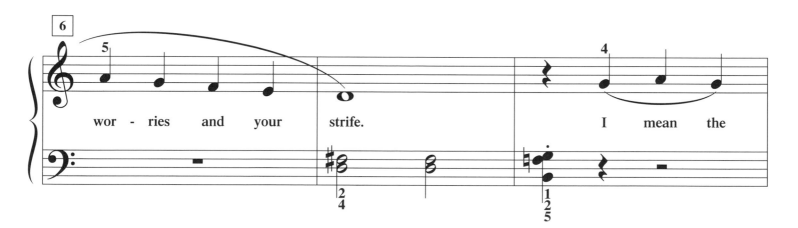

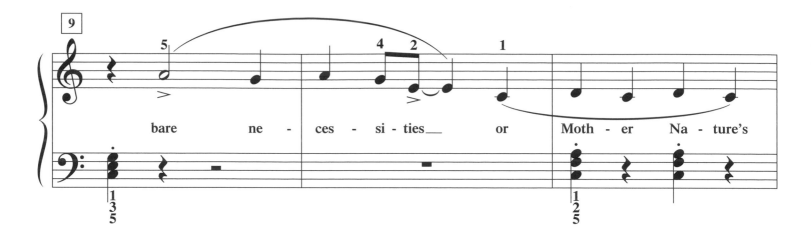

bare ne - ces - si - ties___ or Moth - er Na - ture's

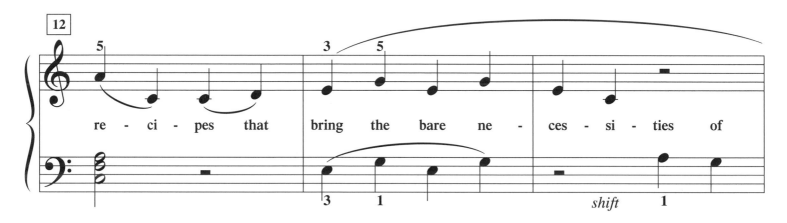

re - ci - pes that bring the bare ne - ces - si - ties of

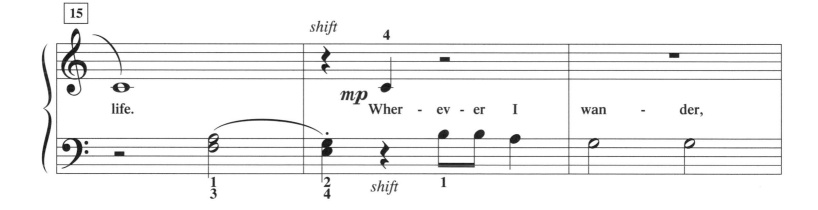

life. Wher - ev - er I wan - der,

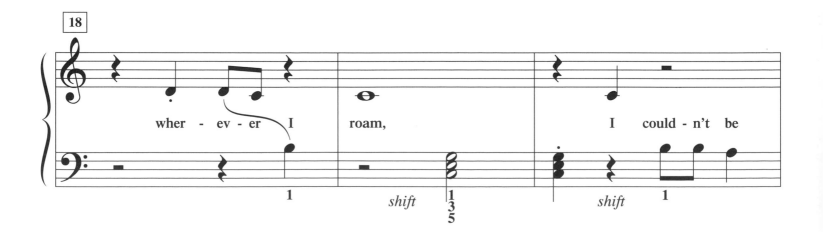

wher - ev - er I roam, I could - n't be

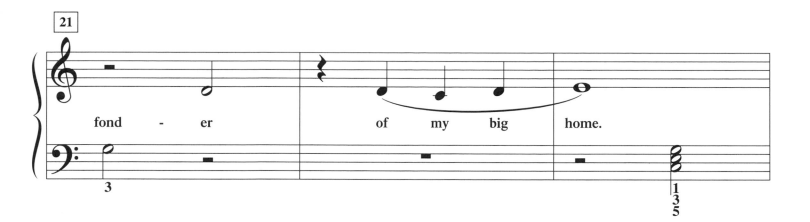

fond - er of my big home.

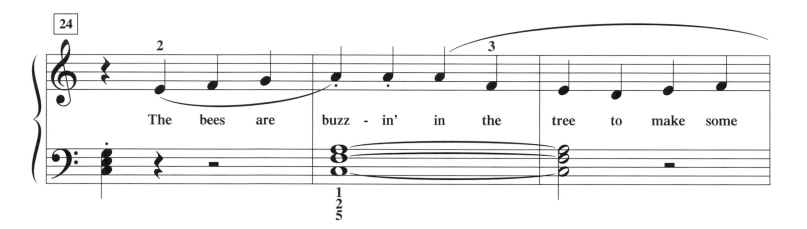

The bees are buzz - in' in the tree to make some

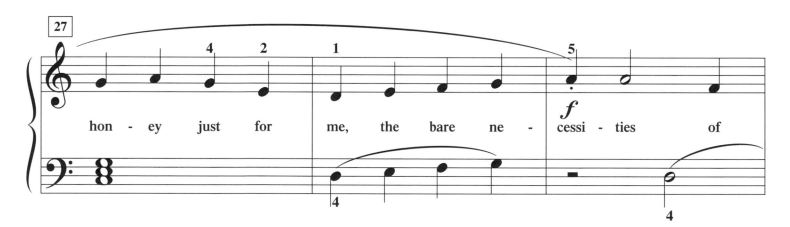

hon - ey just for me, the bare ne - cessi - ties of

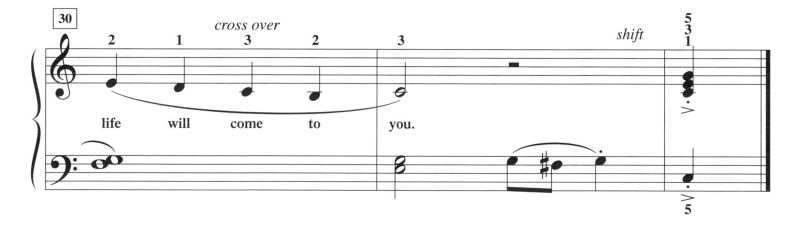

cross over *shift*

life will come to you.

Supercalifragilisticexpialidocious

from *Mary Poppins*

**Words and Music by
Richard M. Sherman
and Robert B. Sherman**

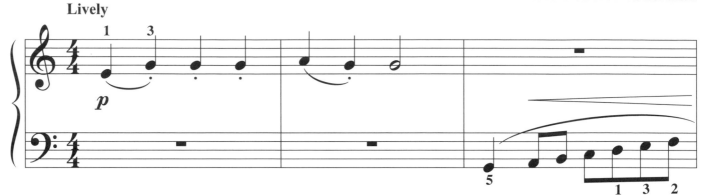

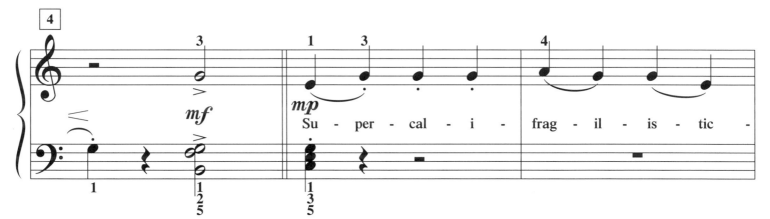

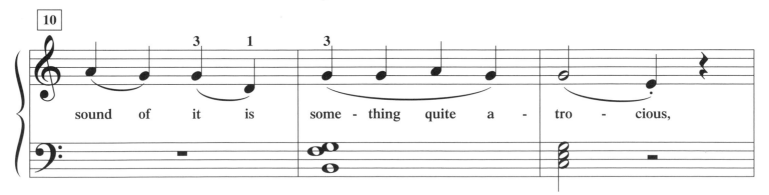

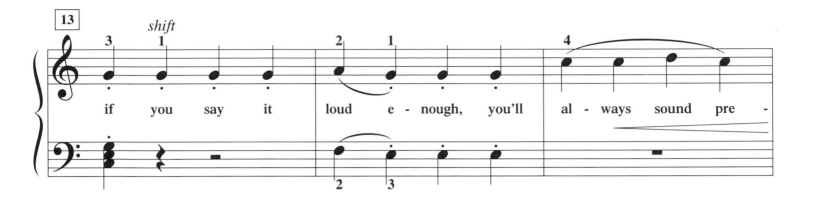

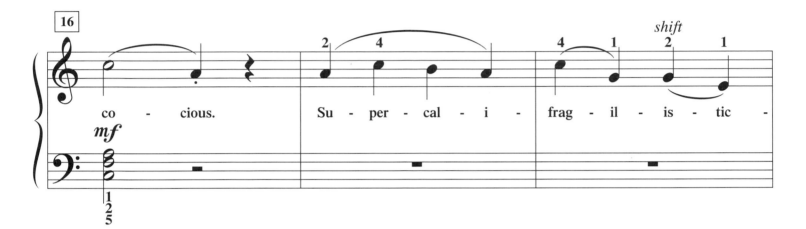

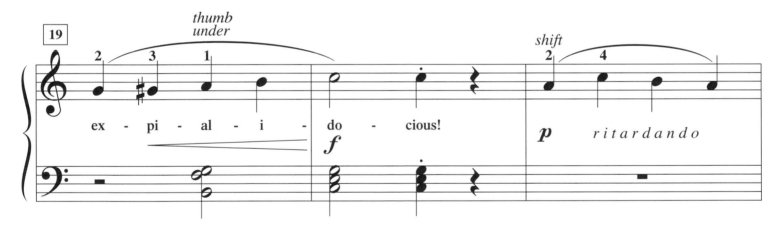

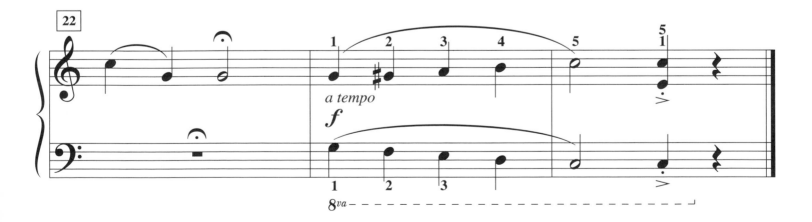

Scales and Arpeggios

from *The Aristocats*

Words and Music by
Richard M. Sherman
and Robert B. Sherman

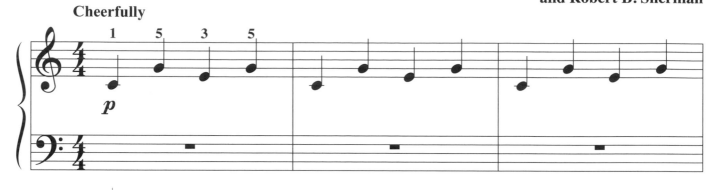

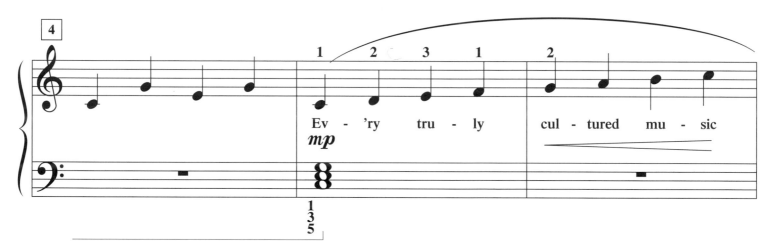

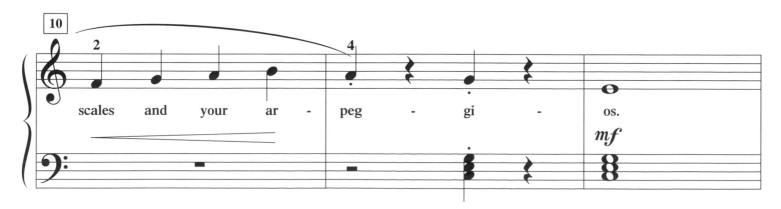

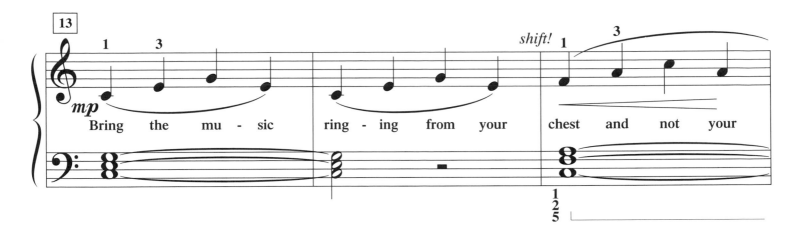

Bring the mu - sic ring - ing from your chest and not your

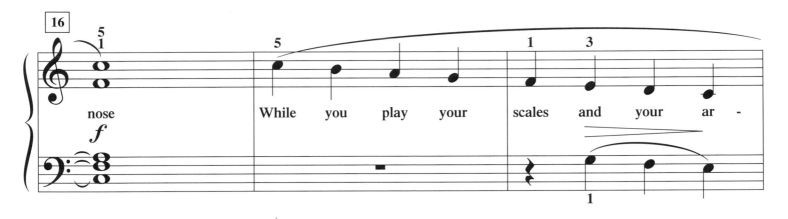

nose While you play your scales and your ar -

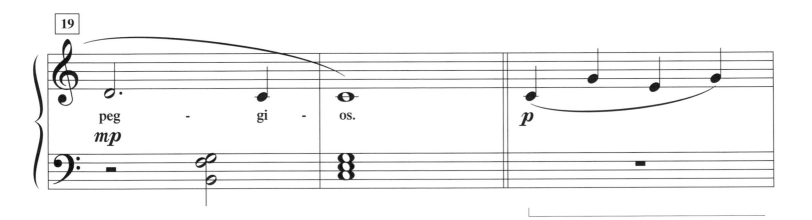

peg - gi - os.

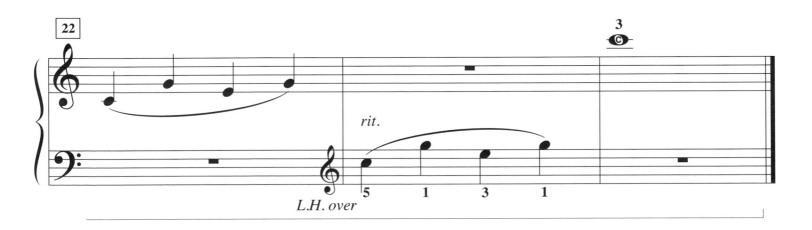

rit.

L.H. over

A Whole New World

from *Aladdin*

Music by Alan Menken
Lyrics by Tim Rice

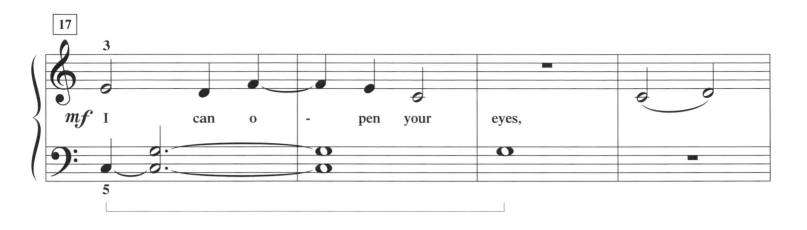

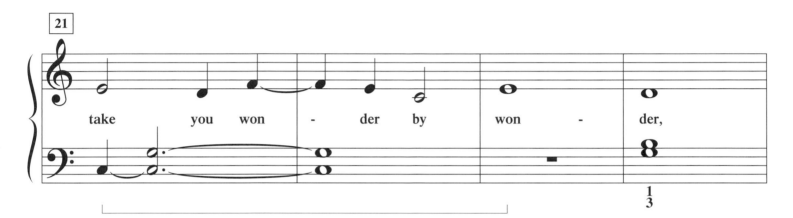

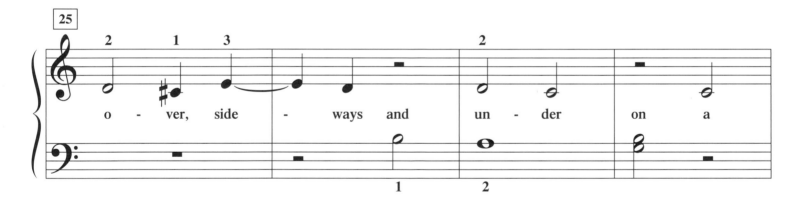

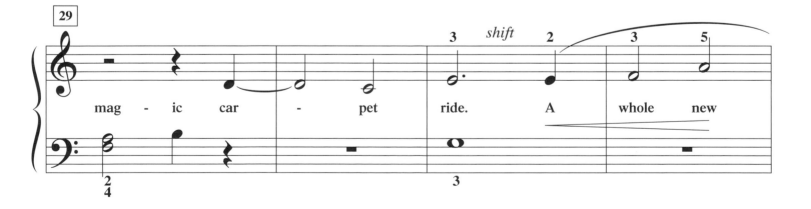

38

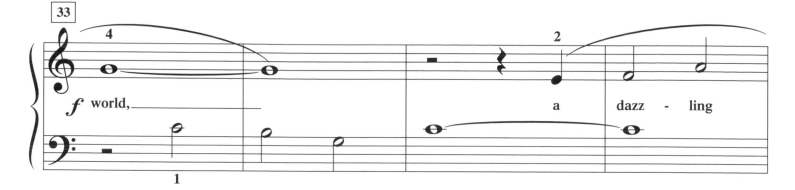

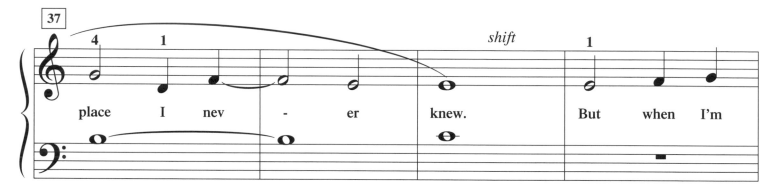

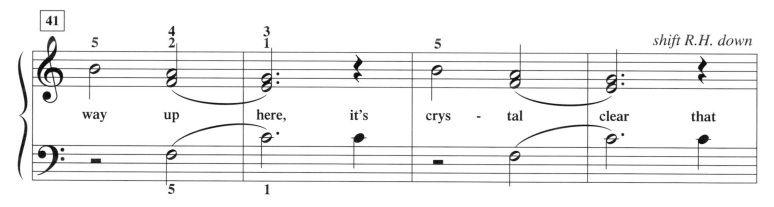

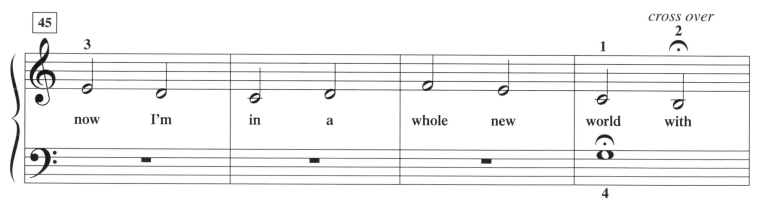

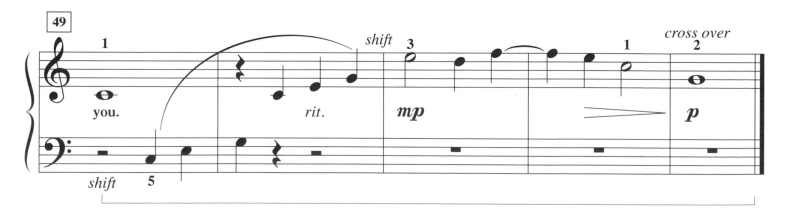

Colors of the Wind

from *Pocahontas*

Music by Alan Menken
Lyrics by Stephen Schwartz

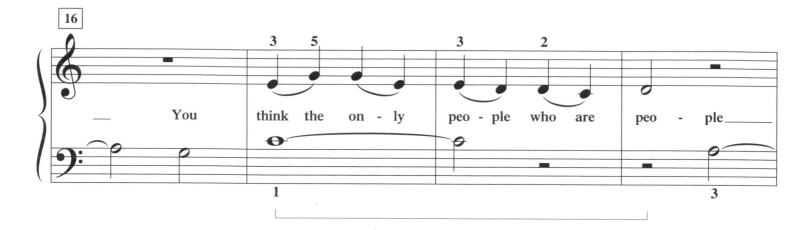

Have you ev - er heard a wolf cry to the blue corn

shift L.H. up to E

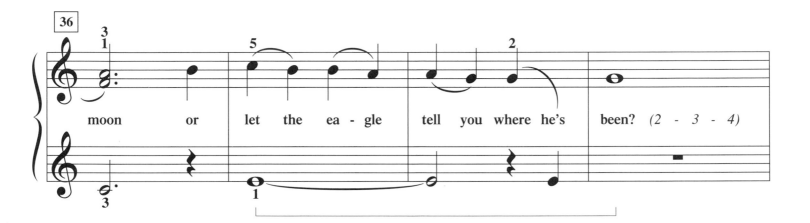

moon or let the ea - gle tell you where he's been? *(2 - 3 - 4)*

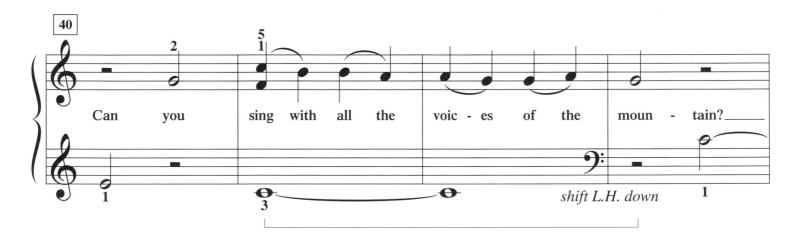

Can you sing with all the voic - es of the moun - tain?____

shift L.H. down

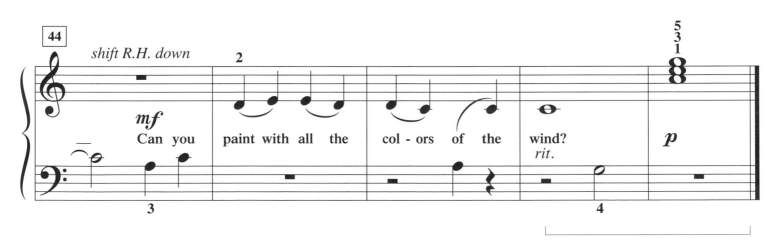

shift R.H. down

Can you paint with all the col - ors of the wind?

rit.

FF3060

Be Our Guest

from *Beauty and the Beast*

Music by Alan Menken
Lyrics by Howard Ashman

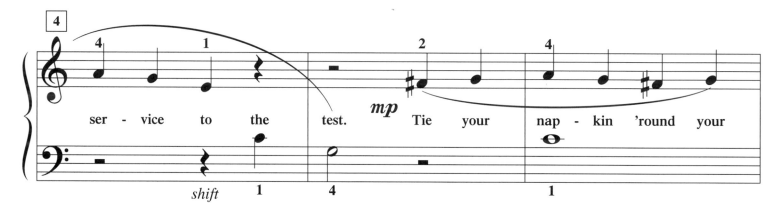

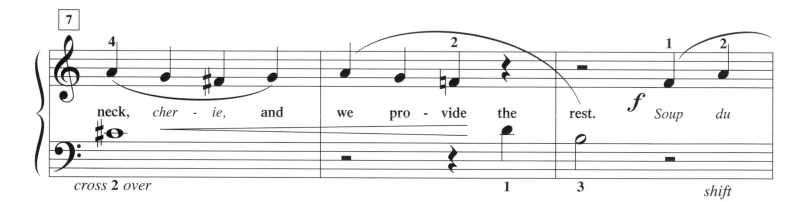

grey stuff. It's de - li - cious! Don't be - lieve me? Ask the

cross 2 over

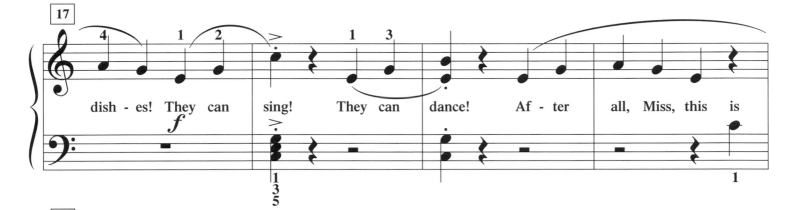

dish - es! They can sing! They can dance! Af - ter all, Miss, this is

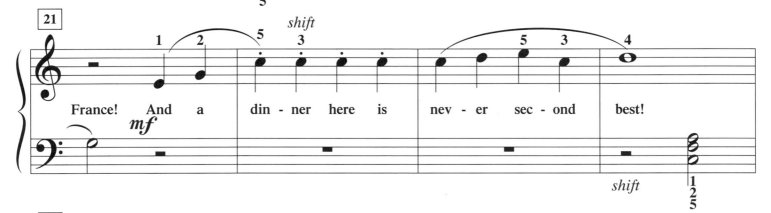

France! And a din - ner here is nev - er sec - ond best!

shift

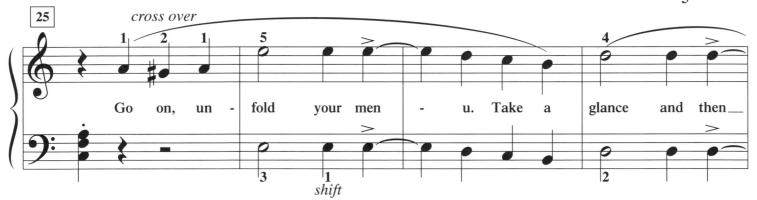

cross over

Go on, un - fold your men - u. Take a glance and then____

shift

____ you'll be our guest! Be our guest! Be our guest!

Belle

from *Beauty and the Beast*

Music by Alan Menken
Lyrics by Howard Ashman

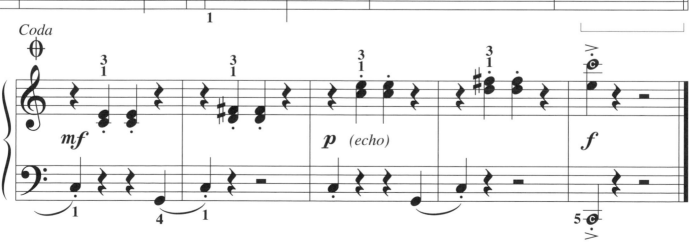

Let It Go
from *Frozen*

Music and Lyrics by
Kristen Anderson-Lopez
and Robert Lopez

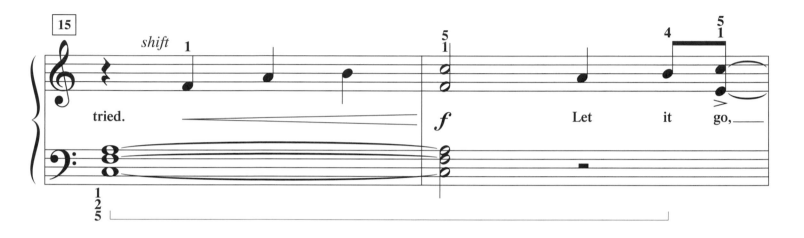

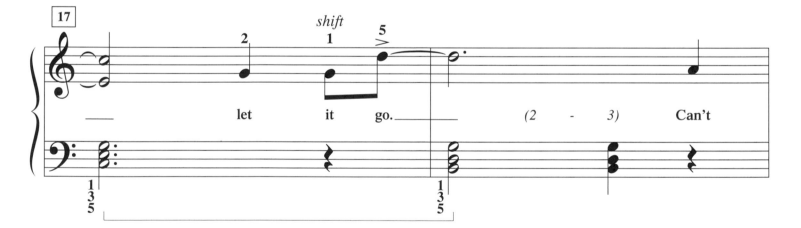

48

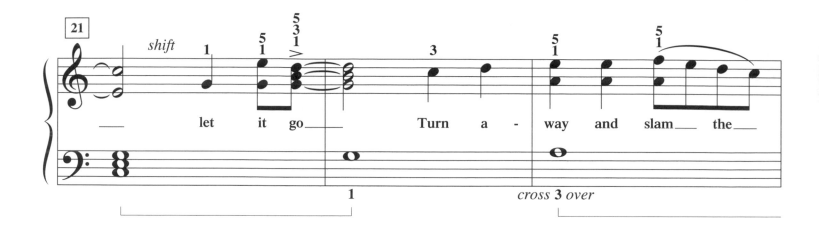

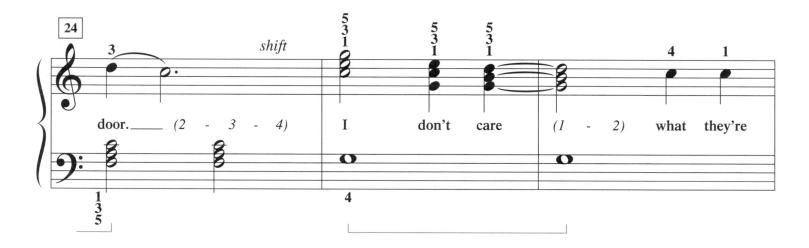

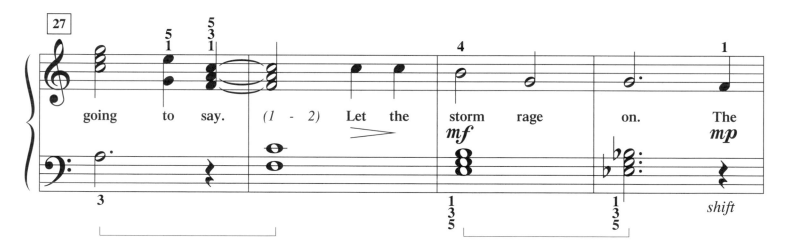

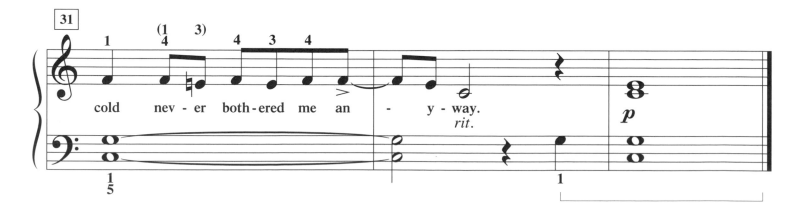

I've Got a Dream

from *Tangled*

Music by Alan Menken
Lyrics by Glenn Slater

FF3060

50

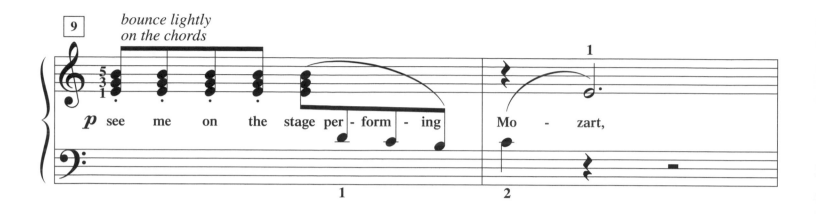

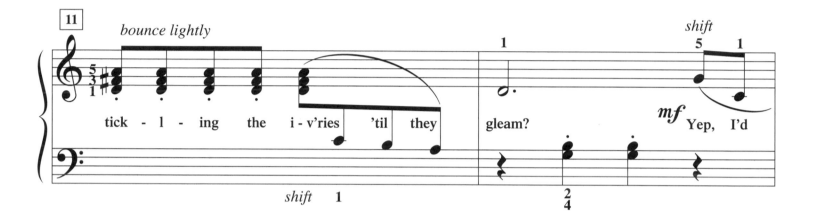

KEY OF G

G Major Scale

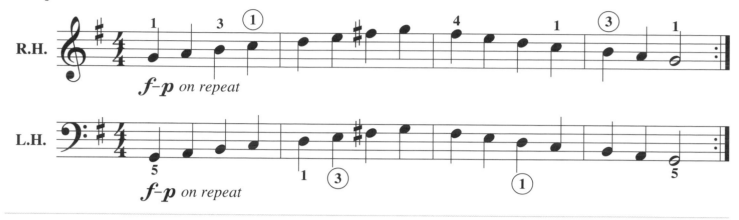

R.H.

f-p on repeat

L.H.

f-p on repeat

Primary Chords in G

REVIEW: The primary chords are built on scale degrees 1, 4, and 5 of the major scale.

NEW: Here are the **I**, **IV**, and **V** chords in the Key of G.

chord letter names: **G**   **C**   **D**

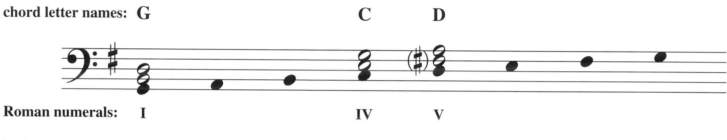

Roman numerals: **I**   **IV**   **V**

In the Key of G the **I**, **IV**, and **V** chords are **G**, **C**, and **D**.

Common Chord Positions

By inverting the notes, the **I**, **IV**, and **V7** chords can be played with little motion of the hand.

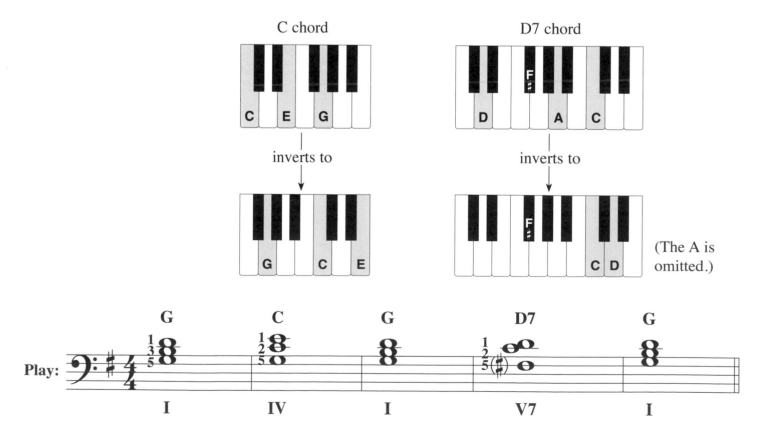

I Just Can't Wait to Be King

from *The Lion King*

Music by Elton John
Lyrics by Tim Rice

FF3060

54

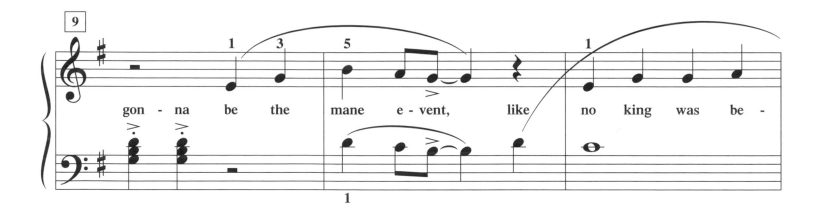

gon - na be the mane e - vent, like no king was be -

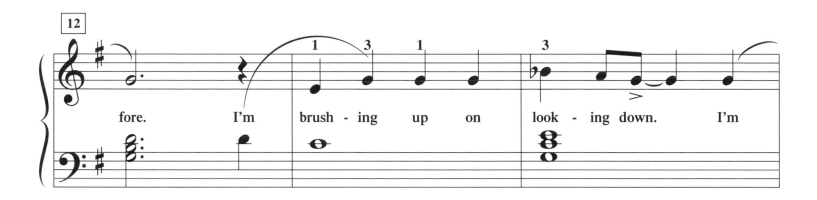

fore. I'm brush - ing up on look - ing down. I'm

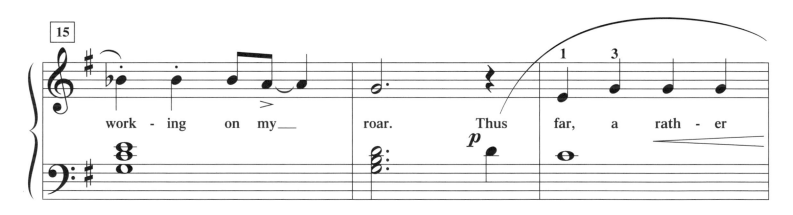

work - ing on my___ roar. Thus far, a rath - er

optional pedal

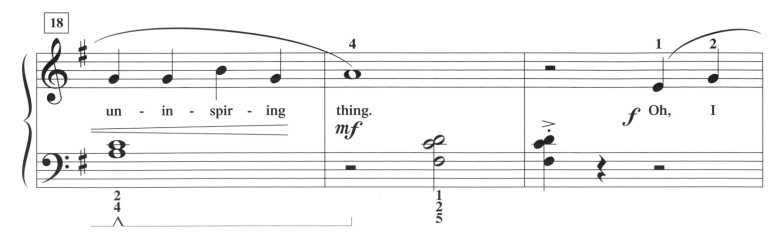

un - in - spir - ing thing. Oh, I

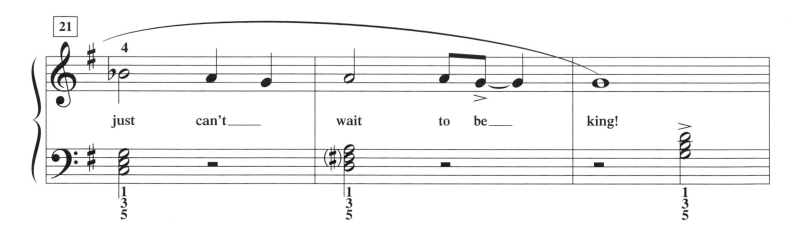

just can't____ wait to be____ king!

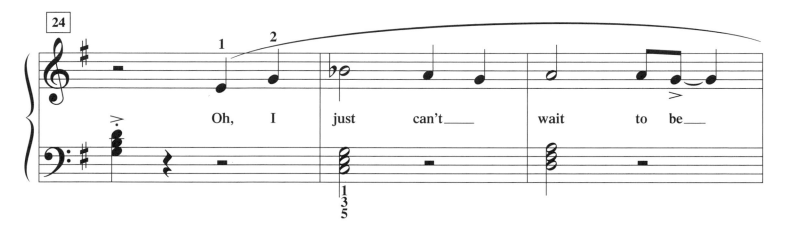

Oh, I just can't____ wait to be____

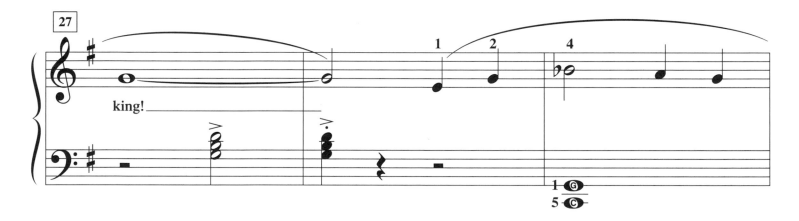

king!_____

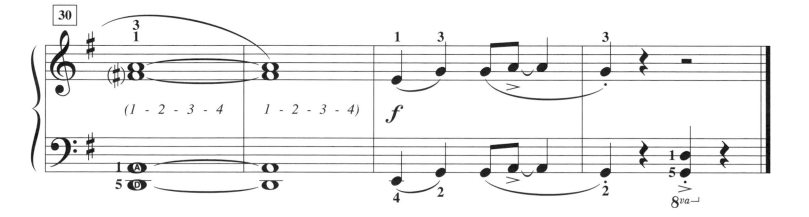

(1 - 2 - 3 - 4 | 1 - 2 - 3 - 4)

f

8va

Under the Sea
from *The Little Mermaid*

Music by Alan Menken
Lyrics by Howard Ashman

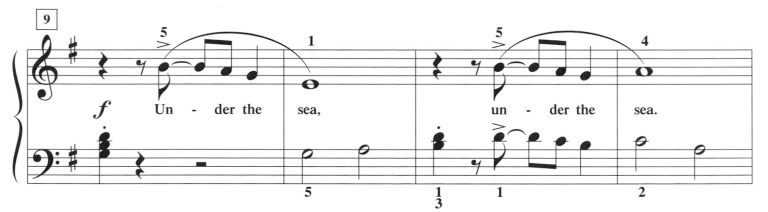

Un - der the sea, un - der the sea.

Dar - lin' it's bet - ter down___where it's wet - ter. Take___ it from

me. Up on the shore they work all day. Out (in) the

sun they slave a - way. While___ we de - vo - tin' full___ time to

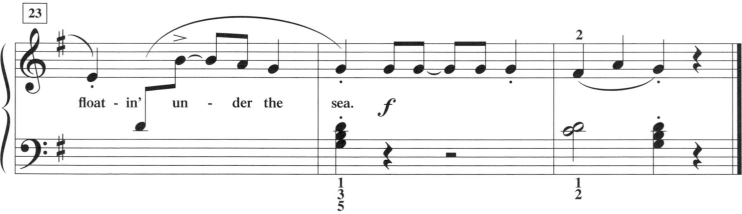

float - in' un - der the sea.

Bella Notte
from *Lady and the Tramp*

**Music and Lyrics by
Peggy Lee and
Sonny Burke**

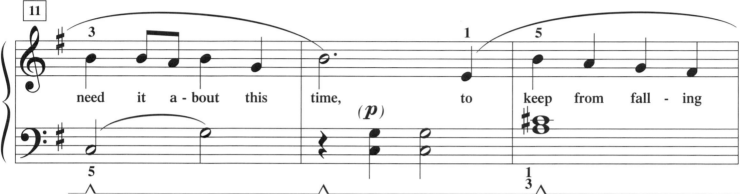

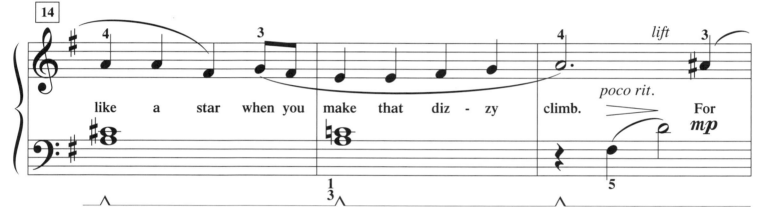

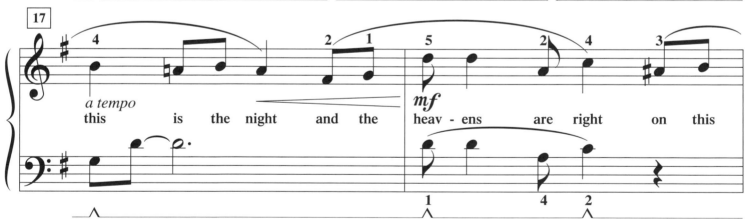

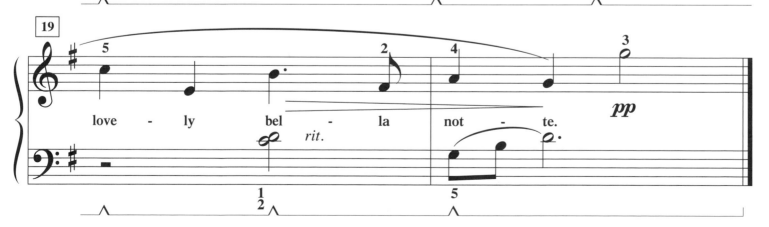

Reflection
from *Mulan*

Music by Matthew Wilder
Words by David Zippel

Can You Feel the Love Tonight

from *The Lion King*

Music by Elton John
Lyrics by Tim Rice

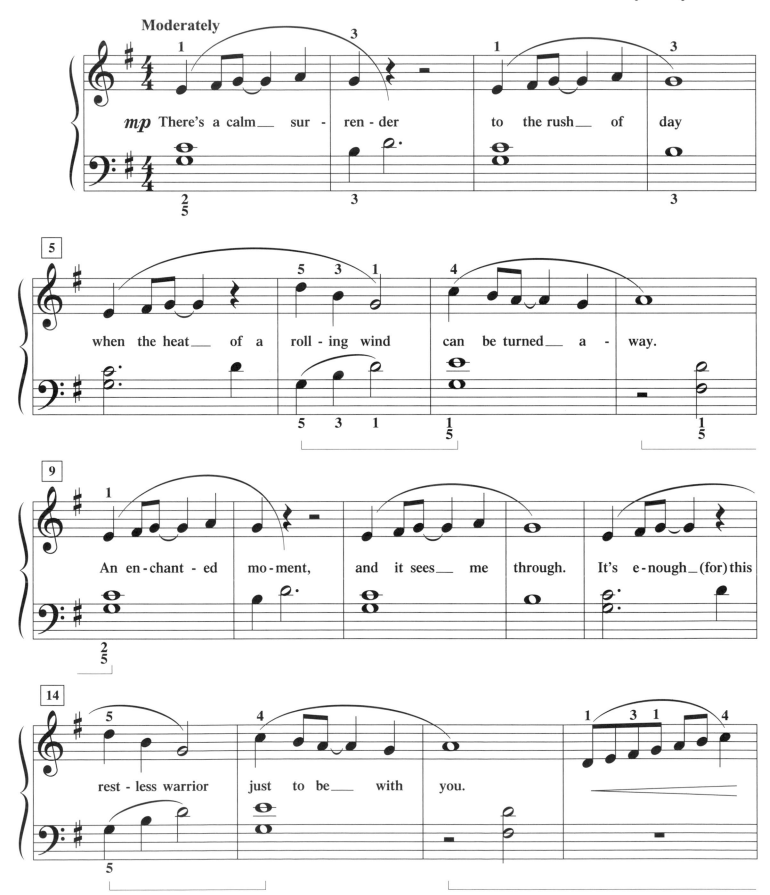

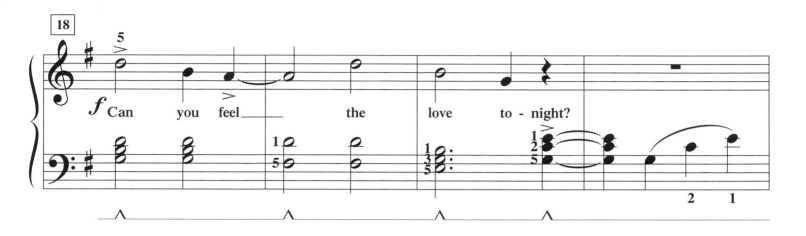

Can you feel the love to - night?

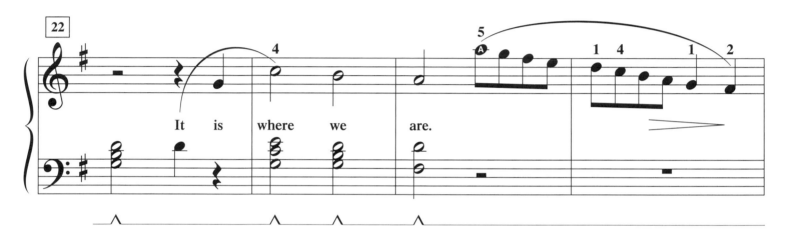

It is where we are.

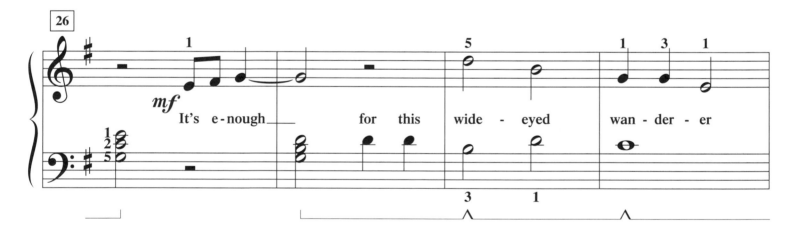

It's e - nough for this wide - eyed wan - der - er

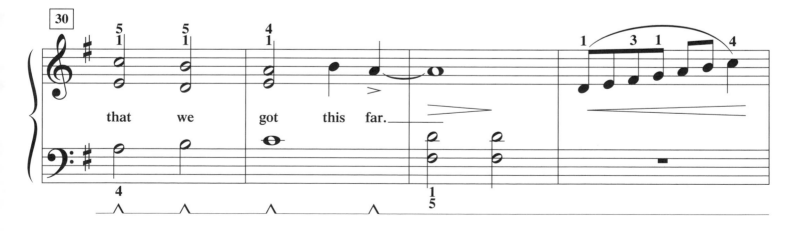

that we got this far.

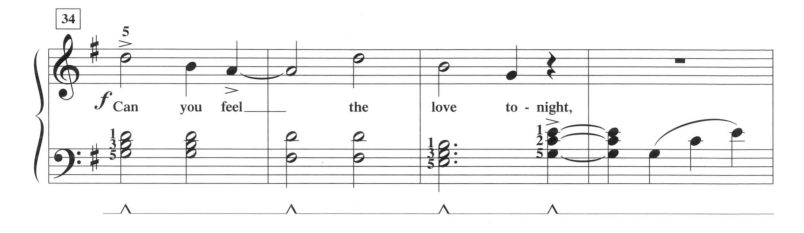

Can you feel the love to - night,

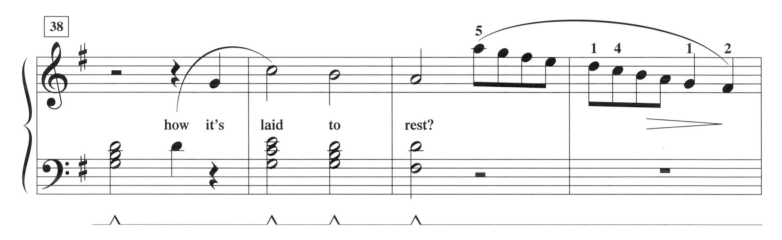

how it's laid to rest?

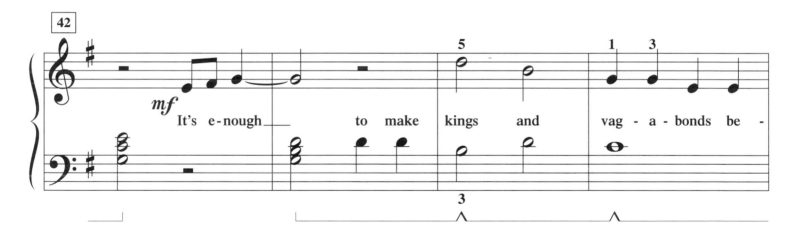

It's e-nough to make kings and vag - a - bonds be -

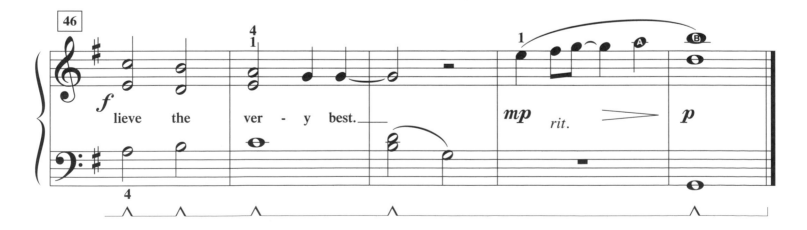

lieve the ver - y best.

Circle of Life
from *The Lion King*

Music by Elton John
Lyrics by Tim Rice

FF3060

far too much to take in here, more to find than can ev - er be

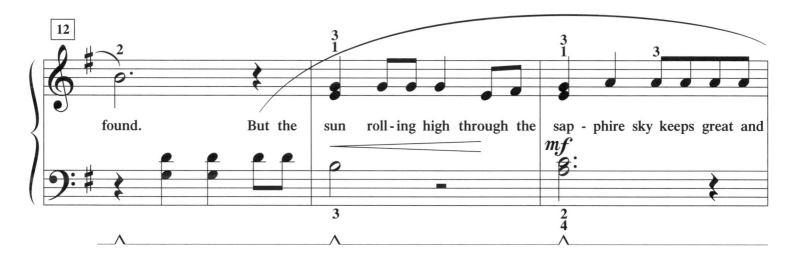

found. But the sun roll-ing high through the sap - phire sky keeps great and

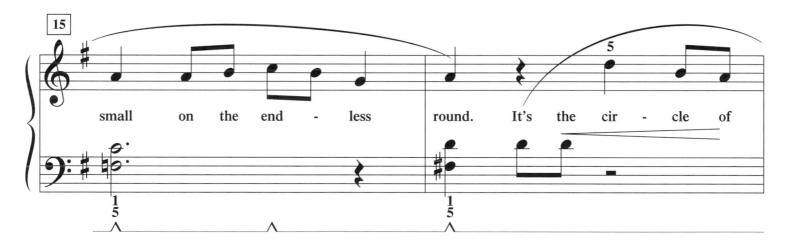

small on the end - less round. It's the cir - cle of

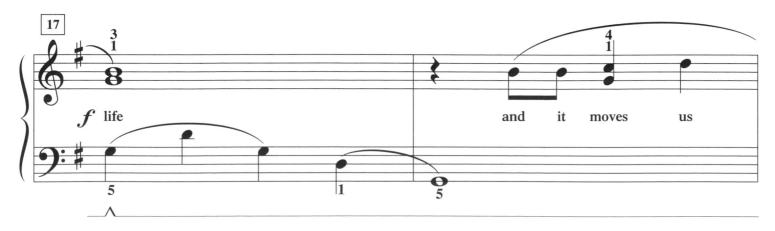

life and it moves us

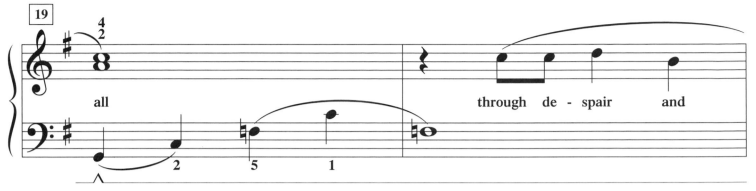

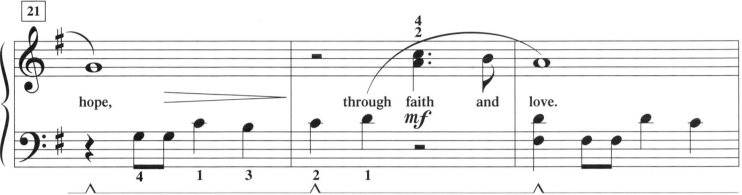

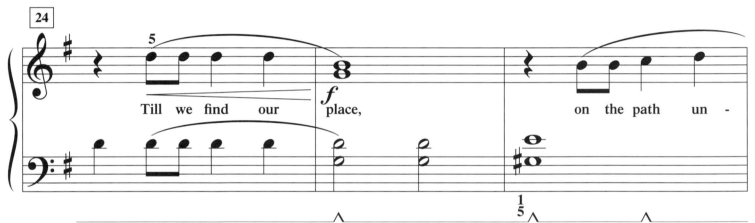

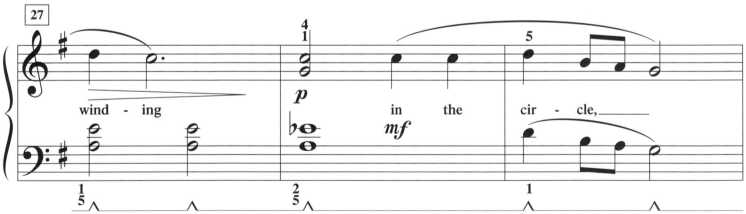

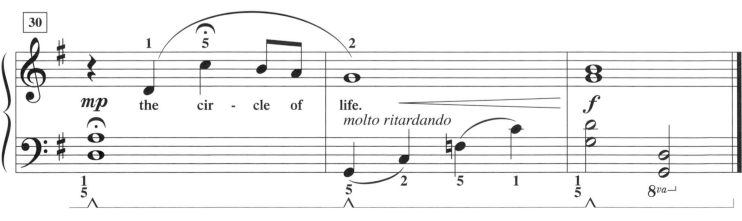

Proud Corazón

from *Coco*

Music by Germaine Franco
Lyrics by Adrian Molina

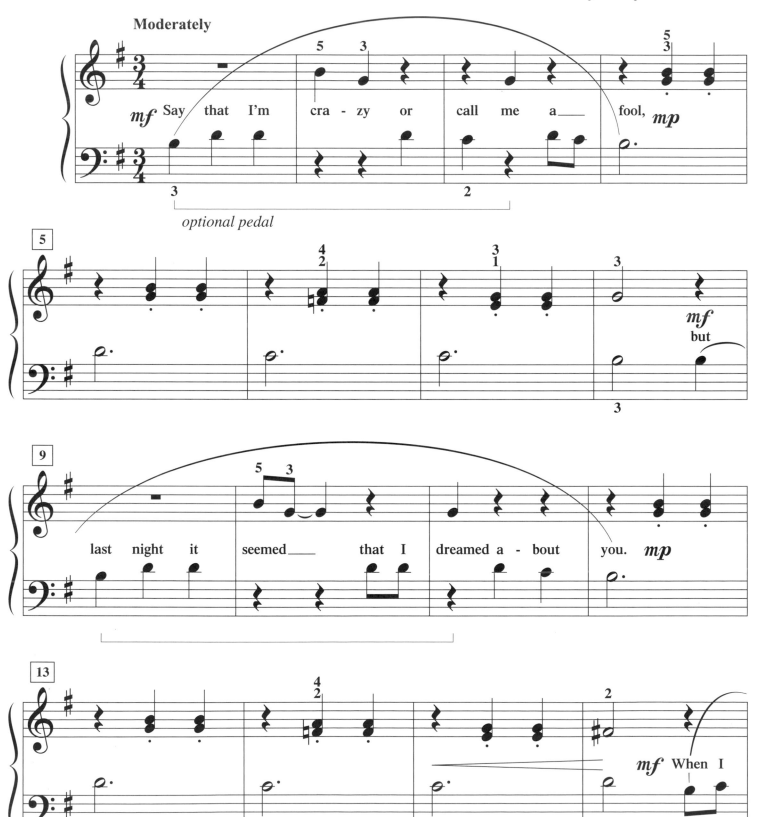

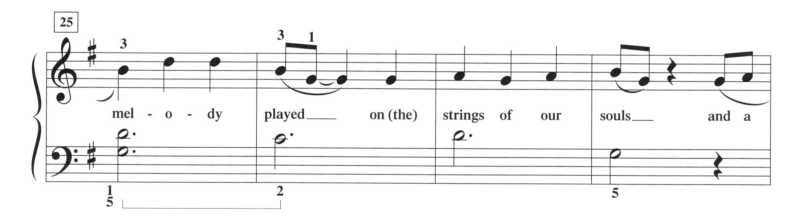

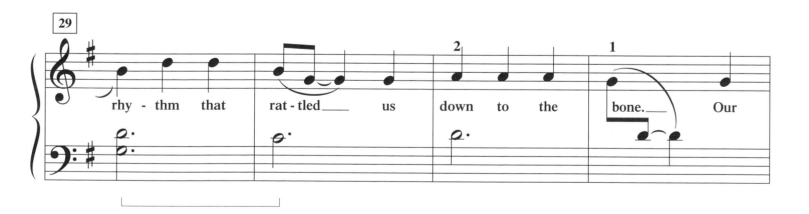

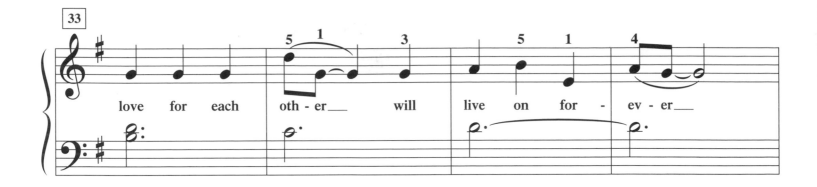

love for each oth - er___ will live on for - ev - er___

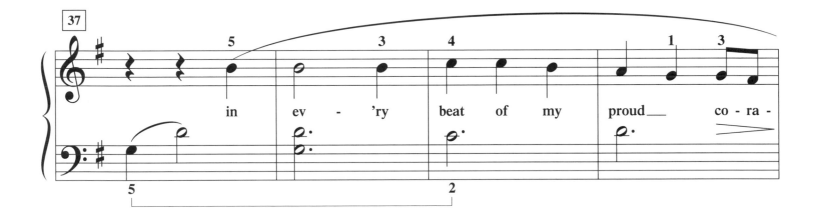

in ev - 'ry beat of my proud___ co - ra -

zón. *rit.* shift both hands to A position *a tempo* ¡Ay! Mi fa -

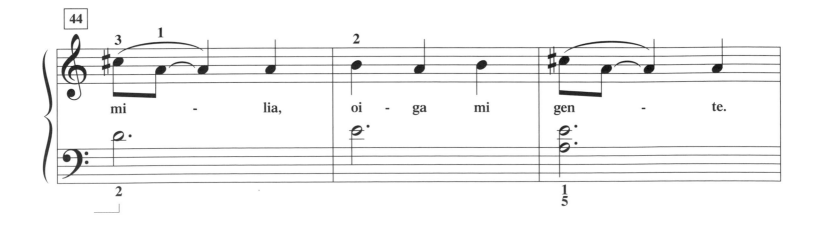

mi - lia, oi - ga mi gen - te.

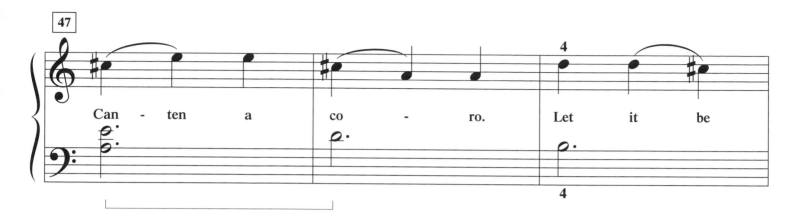

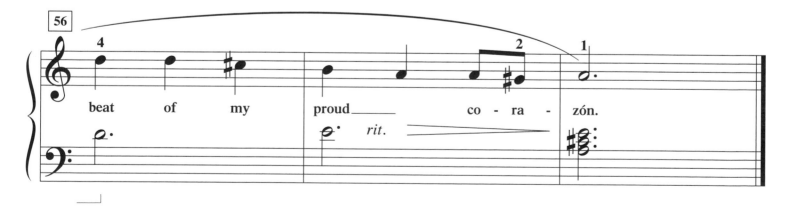

Fathoms Below

from *The Little Mermaid*

Music by Alan Menken
Lyrics by Howard Ashman

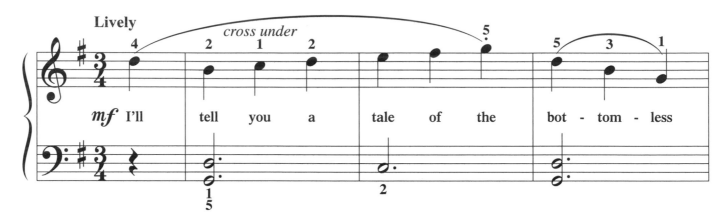

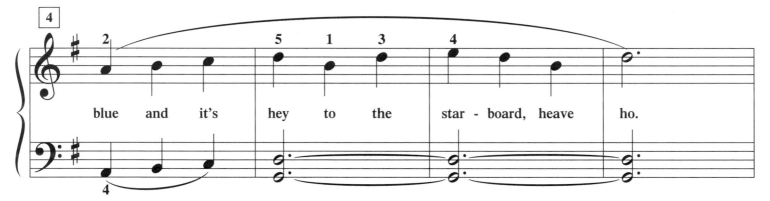

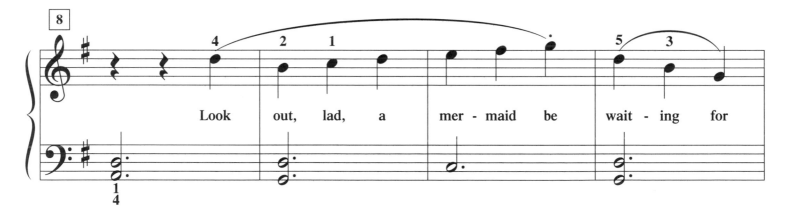

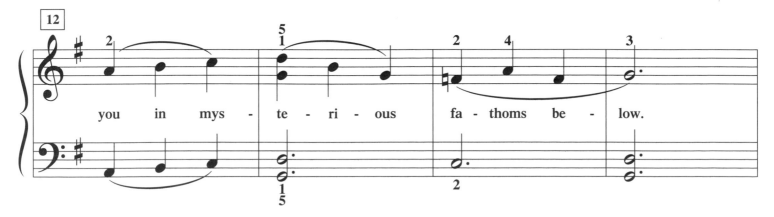

FF3060

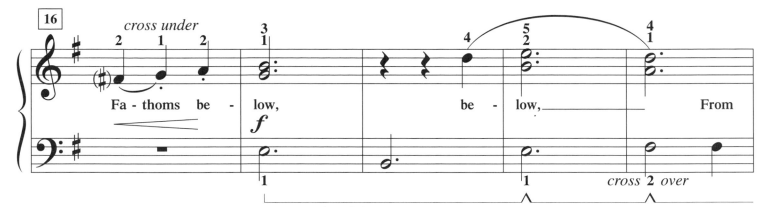

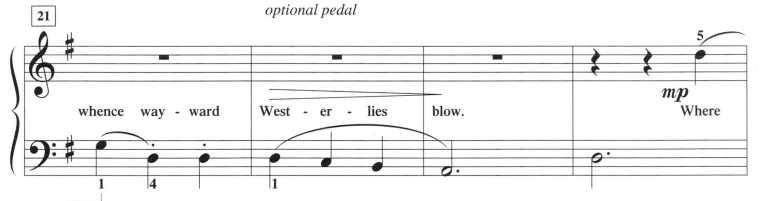

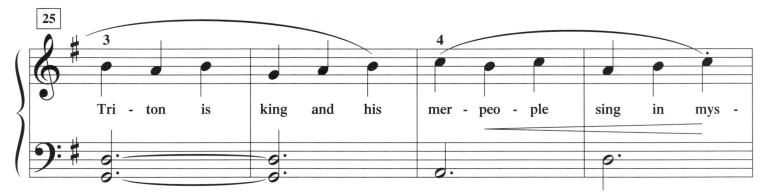

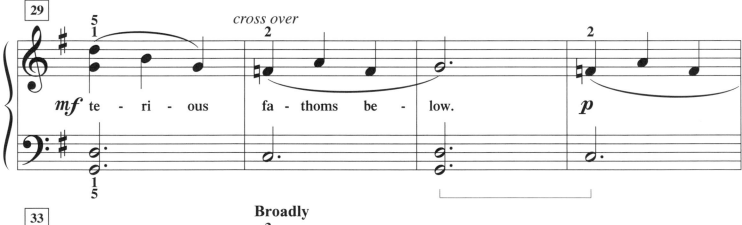

Beauty and the Beast

from *Beauty and the Beast*

Music by Alan Menken
Lyrics by Howard Ashman

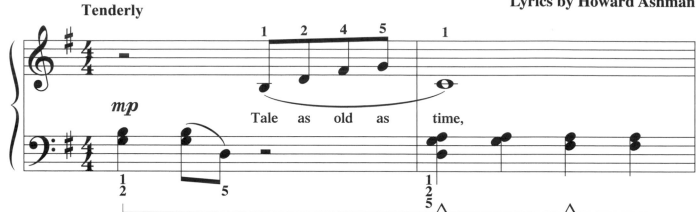

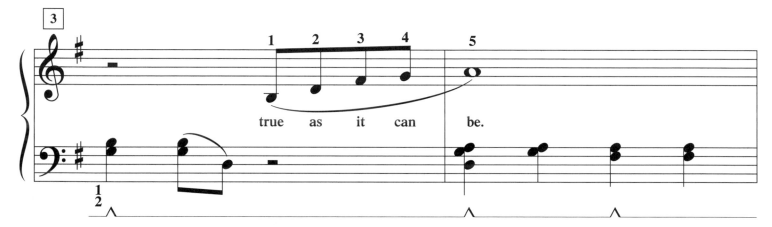

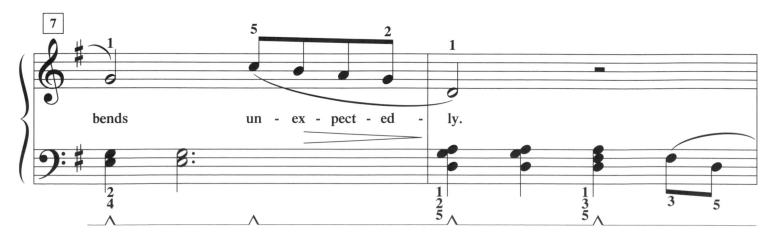

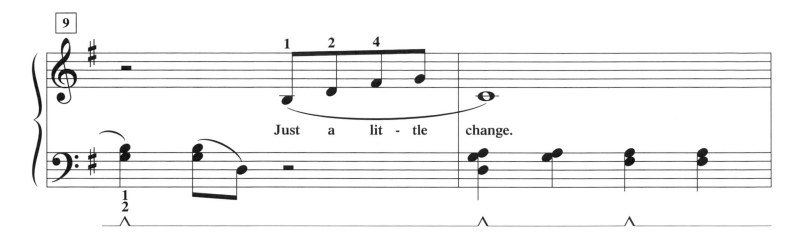

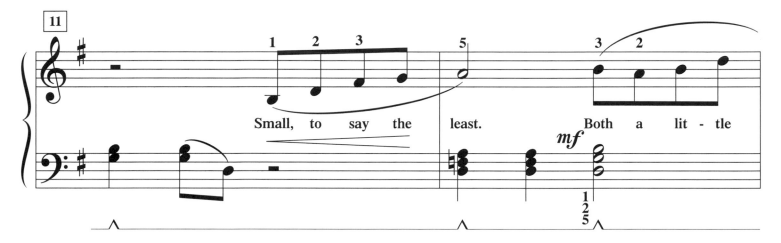

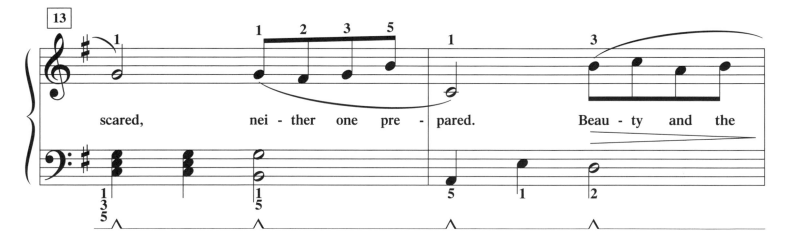

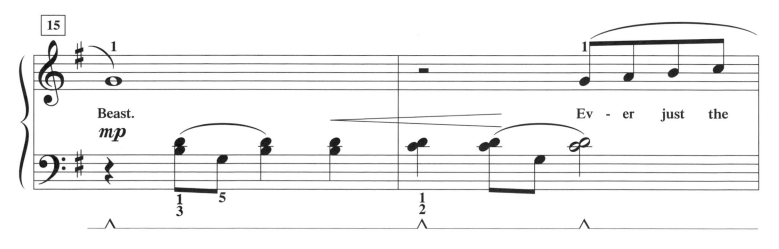

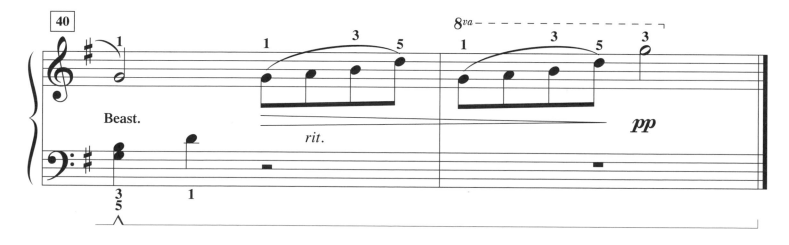

DICTIONARY OF MUSICAL TERMS

DYNAMIC MARKS

pp	**p**	**mp**	**mf**	**f**	**ff**
pianissimo	*piano*	*mezzo piano*	*mezzo forte*	*forte*	*fortissimo*
very soft	soft	moderately soft	moderately loud	loud	very loud

crescendo (cresc.)
Play gradually louder.

diminuendo (dim.) or decrescendo (decresc.)
Play gradually softer.

SIGN	TERM	DEFINITION
	accent mark	Play this note louder.
	accidental	Sharps, flats, or naturals added to a piece and not in the key signature.
	C major chord	A three-note chord built in 3rds above C: C-E-G.
	C major scale	An eight-note scale (C-D-E-F-G-A-B-C) with half steps between scale steps 3-4 and 7-8.
	chord	Three or more tones sounding together.
	I ("one") chord	The Roman numeral I indicates the triad built on scale degree 1.
	IV ("four")	The Roman numeral IV indicates the triad built on scale degree 4.
	V7 ("five-seven")	A four-note chord built up in 3rds from scale degree 5 (often played with only three notes).
	chord symbol	The letter name of a chord (shown above the staff) indicating the harmony.
	coda	Ending section.
	D7 chord	A four-note chord built up in 3rds from D (D-F#-A-C). The notes of the D7 chord are often inverted to form a 3-note D7 chord.
D.C. al Coda	**Da Capo al Coda**	Return to the beginning and play to ⊕ , then jump to the *Coda* (ending).
	damper pedal	The right pedal, which sustains the sound, played with the right foot.
	dotted half note	Three counts or beats.
	eighth notes	Two eighth notes equal one quarter note.
	fermata	Hold this note longer than its normal value.
	fifth (5th)	The interval of a 5th spans five letter names. (Ex. C up to G, or A down to D) Line-(skip-a-line)-line, or space-(skip-a-space)-space.
♭	**flat**	A flat lowers a note one half step.
	fourth (4th)	The interval of a 4th spans four letter names. (Ex. C up to F, or G down to D) Line-(skip-a-line)-space, or space-(skip-a-space)-line.
	G major chord	A three-note chord built in 3rds above G: G-B-D. G is the root. B is the 3rd. D is the 5th.
	G major scale	An eight-note scale (G-A-B-C-D-E-F#-G) with half steps between scale degrees 3-4 and 7-8.
	G7 chord	A four-note chord built up in 3rds from G (G-B-D-F). The notes of the G7 chord are often inverted to form a 3-note G7 chord.
	half note	Two counts or beats (one-half the value of a whole note).
	half rest	Two counts of silence. (Sits on line 3 of the staff.)

	half step	The distance from one key to the very closest key on the keyboard. (Ex. C-C♯, or E-F)
	interval	The distance between two musical tones, keys on the keyboard, or notes on the staff. (Ex. 2nd, 3rd, 4th, 5th)
	key signature	The key signature appears at the beginning of each line of music. It indicates sharps or flats to be used throughout the piece.
	ledger line	A short line used to extend the staff.
	legato	Smooth, connected.
	major scale	An eight-note scale with half steps between scale degrees 3-4 and 7-8.
	molto	Much, very.
	natural	A natural (always a white key) cancels a sharp or a flat.
	octave	The interval which spans 8 letter names. (Ex. C to C)
	ottava	Play one octave higher (or lower) than written.
	pedal change	Shows the down-up motion of the damper pedal.
	phrase	A musical sentence. A phrase is often shown by a slur, also called a phrase mark.
	primary chords	The I, IV, and V chords are the primary chords in any major key.
	quarter note	One count or beat. (One-quarter the value of a whole note.)
	quarter rest	One beat of silence.
	repeat sign	Play the music within the repeat signs again.
	ritardando	Gradually slowing down.
	root position	The letter name of the chord is the lowest note.
	scale	From the Latin word *scala*, meaning "ladder." The notes of a scale move up or down by 2nds (steps).
	second (2nd) (step)	The interval that spans two letter names. (Ex. C up to D, or F down to E) On the staff: line-to-the-next-space or space-to-the-next-line.
	sharp	A sharp raises the note one half step.
	sixth (6th)	The interval that spans six letter names. (Ex. E up to C, or D down to F) On the staff a 6th is written line-(skip 2 lines)-space or space-(skip 2 spaces)-line.
	slur	A curved line that indicates legato playing.
	staccato	Detached, disconnected.
	tempo	The speed of the music.
	**third (3rd) (skip)**	The interval that spans three letter names. (Ex. C up to E, or F down to D) On the staff: line-to-the-next-line or space-to-the-next-space.
	tie	A curved line that connects two notes on the same line or space. Hold for the total counts of both notes.
	time signature	Two numbers at the beginning of a piece (one above the other). The top number indicates the number of beats per measure; the bottom number represents the note receiving the beat.
	triad	A 3-note chord built in 3rds.
	upbeat (pick-up note)	The note(s) of an incomplete opening measure.
	whole note	Four counts or beats.
	whole rest	Silence for any whole measure. (Hangs below line 4.)
	whole step	The distance of two half steps.

ALPHABETICAL INDEX OF TITLES

The Bare Necessities (from *The Jungle Book*) 29

Beauty and the Beast (from *Beauty and the Beast*) 74

Bella Notte (from *Lady and the Tramp*) 58

Belle (from *Beauty and the Beast*) 44

Be Our Guest (from *Beauty and the Beast*) 42

Can You Feel the Love Tonight (from *The Lion King*) 62

Chim Chim Cher-ee (from *Mary Poppins*) 24

Circle of Life (from *The Lion King*) 65

Colors of the Wind (from *Pocahontas*) 39

Do You Want to Build a Snowman? (from *Frozen*) 4

Fathoms Below (from *The Little Mermaid*) 72

Gaston (from *Beauty and the Beast*) 18

He's a Pirate (from *Pirates of the Caribbean*) 26

I Just Can't Wait to Be King (from *The Lion King*) 53

I See the Light (from *Tangled*) 6

It's a Small World (from Disney Parks' "it's a small world" Attraction) . . 12

I've Got a Dream (from *Tangled*) 49

Let It Go (from *Frozen*) 46

Let's Go Fly a Kite (from *Mary Poppins*) 16

Part of Your World (from *The Little Mermaid*) 10

Proud Corazón (from *Coco*) 68

Reflection (from *Mulan*) 60

Remember Me (Ernesto de la Cruz) (from *Coco*) 22

Scales and Arpeggios (from *The Aristocats*) 34

A Spoonful of Sugar (from *Mary Poppins*) 14

Step in Time (from *Mary Poppins*) 8

Supercalifragilisticexpialidocious (from *Mary Poppins*) 32

Under the Sea (from *The Little Mermaid*) 56

A Whole New World (from *Aladdin*) 36